Woman's Day

DOUGHCRAFTS

WOMAN'S DAY
DOUGH CRAFTS

LORRAINE BODGER

illustrated by
Lorraine Bodger

Sedgewood™ Press
NEW YORK

For CBS Inc.

Editorial Director: *Dina von Zweck*

Project Coordinator: *Ruth Josimovich*

For Sedgewood™ Press

Editorial Director, Sedgewood™ Press: *Jane Ross*

Project Director: *Virginia Colton*

Managing Editor: *Gale Kremer*

Designer: *Bentwood Studio/Jos. Trautwein*

Production Manager: *Bill Rose*

Photography: *Robert Epstein*

I would like to express my appreciation to Robert Epstein, photographer, and Jos. Trautwein, book designer, for everything they did to make this book look so special.

Thanks also to the American Tree and Wreath Company for generously allowing us to use some of their fine products.

Distributed in the Trade by Van Nostrand Reinhold.
ISBN 0-442-28180-3
Library of Congress Catalog Number 83-60325
Manufactured in the United States of America.

Introduction

IT SEEMS STRANGE to be writing the introduction after the rest of the book has been completed. But here I am, thinking back on the past months of working on doughcraft, trying to introduce it to you and trying to wrap it all up for me. I remember that I thought it was going to be fun from the minute I started on the book in late summer—fun to knead and squeeze and shape and play with dough. I knew it would be a pleasure to experiment and invent new projects and decorate them and paint them.

It was wonderful in many unexpected ways, too. I had a couple of weeks of brilliant autumn weather on Long Island, making sugar paste projects and watching the light and the leaves change. I spent the Christmas holidays working on the holiday projects for the book. I was warm and cozy, finishing up the projects and working on the photography, during the snow and cold of a New York winter. And while the chilly spring rain went on and on outside, I sat at my desk and wrote the manuscript and made the drawings. So it seems to me in May that I have had quite a full measure from this book—fun, satisfaction, pride, a chance to play. And now it gives me a great deal of pleasure to put it in your hands.

LORRAINE BODGER

 # CONTENTS

2 Baskets, Bowls, Centerpieces and Wall Pieces   41

3 Christmas Decorations   77

4 Thanksgiving, Valentine's Day and Easter   123

5 Projects for Children of All Ages 149

The Basics of Doughcraft

In this chapter you will find the practical information you need for doing the doughcraft projects. All the recipes are here, as well as techniques for working with the different doughs, how to color or paint the doughs, baking and finishing methods, trouble-shooting tips, what equipment you'll need and how to use it.

FLOUR/SALT DOUGH

This dough is incredibly versatile, as you can see from the variety of projects in this book. With it, you can work as small as the Kitten Napkin Rings on page 124 or as large as Old MacDonald's Farm on page 150. You can leave the dough unpainted, as in the Cookie Wreath on page 119, or paint it in brilliant colors, like the Mexican Candleholders on page 47. Your project can be as plain and simple as the Bread Basket on page 64 or as jazzy as the Tree-of-Life Wall Piece on page 70.

The basic process is simple: Mix flour and salt, add water and knead until the dough is smooth. Then you can roll the dough flat and cut it, roll strands and coil them, model the dough by hand, weave it, layer it, mold it over foundations. Keep whatever part of the dough you're not using wrapped tightly in plastic; you can store tightly wrapped leftovers in the refrigerator for up to a week.

Note: Although the dough is made of flour, salt and water, it is not edible.

Ingredients:

> 4 cups white flour
> 1 cup salt (iodized or plain)
> 1½ cups water

In a big bowl, mix the flour and salt until well blended and smooth. Add 1 cup of the water and continue to mix. Slowly add the remaining ½ cup water, turning the dough in the bowl. Push the dough into a ball, working in any dry flour and salt left at the bottom of the bowl. Knead on a floured surface for at least 10 minutes. Wrap the dough tightly in plastic.

Tip: You can cut the ball of dough in half and knead each half separately for 10 minutes. Be sure to keep the half you're not kneading wrapped in plastic.

There are only two problems you might have when you make the dough: It might be too dry or it might be too moist. You will know if it is dry because the edges will split and crack every time you push the heel of your hand into the dough during the kneading process, even after a few minutes of kneading when the dough should be holding together. To counteract the dryness, simply wet your hands and continue kneading, working the moisture into the dough. You may have to repeat this several times, but go slowly—don't overdo it or you'll end up with problem No. 2, moist or weepy dough.

When you hold a ball of weepy dough, it seems to ooze away between your fingers. It's just too moist to hold a shape. The antidote is to add flour *and* salt. Mix ¼ cup of flour with ¼ cup of salt and dust your kneading surface with this mixture. As you knead, the flour/salt mixture will be incorporated into the dough. Continue to dust and knead until the dough has firmed up. Don't overdo this either, or you'll be back with problem No. 1.

It is important to remember that this type of dough is, in general, all too responsive to changes in humidity and temperature. You may make the dough exactly the same way on two different days and get two totally different results. Don't worry about it. Just correct any problem as recommended above and go on with your project. Remember, also, that the problem sometimes isn't a problem: Woven baskets, like the Planter Basket on page 42, require a somewhat dry, stiff dough so the woven strips don't stretch; the lion and lamb Christmas ornaments on page 101 demand a softer dough for the garlic-pressed mane and fleece.

A note of caution: Don't use old dough for your projects. You can store the tightly wrapped unused portion of dough in the refrigerator and continue to use it up to about a week. (Bring it to room temperature before working with it.) But after a week, throw it out and make a new batch. Dough behaves unpredictably after a week and you won't want to risk putting time and effort into a project that may be ruined because the dough was too old.

On the matter of size, your projects must necessarily be limited to the dimensions of a shelf in your oven. All the projects in this book fit onto a shelf 15″ wide and 18″ deep. But even more important, the projects fit onto heavy-duty cookie sheets measuring 11½″ × 16½″. You can, of course, bake separate items on two cookie sheets, one sheet on each shelf of the oven.

BASIC EQUIPMENT FOR FLOUR / SALT DOUGH PROJECTS

These are the items needed most often. Other materials necessary for specific projects are indicated at the beginning of each project.

Rolling pin
Heavy-duty cookie sheets
Wire racks (for cooling)
Small spatula, long spatula
Sharp knife
Ruler
Wooden skewers and round toothpicks
Satin-finish polyurethane, turpentine, brush
White glue, epoxy glue
Plastic straws
Acrylic paints, brushes
Large and small cookie cutters
Aspic cutters

NINE BASIC TECHNIQUES FOR SHAPING
FLOUR / SALT DOUGH

1. Roll the dough into strands and braid it. (*Example:* Braided Wreath Ornament, page 86.)

Break off a piece of dough and roll it back and forth on a flour-dusted surface to make a long strand, anywhere from ¼″ to 1″ in diameter. Repeat to make two more strands. Transfer the strands to the flour-dusted back of a cookie sheet and braid them together, being careful not to stretch the dough as you braid. Shape the braids according to the project instructions, cut off the excess dough and join the ends together, moistening them with water.

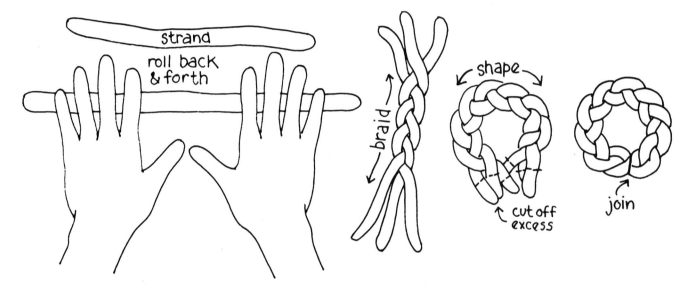

2. Roll the dough into strands and form them into a flat shape. (*Examples:* Tree-of-Life Wall Piece, page 70; Openwork Bird Ornament, page 86.)

Roll a strand as explained above and transfer it to the flour-dusted back of a cookie sheet. Shape the strand according to the project's requirements, adding strands as needed. Moisten and join the ends.

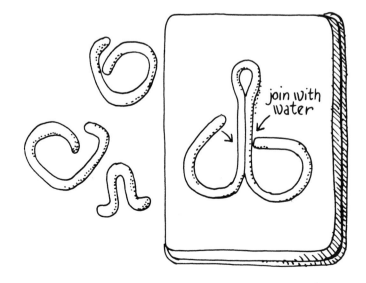

3. Roll the dough into strands and coil them around an ovenproof foundation. (*Example:* Fruit Bowl, page 60.)

The foundation must be shaped in such a way that the dough can be slipped off after baking.

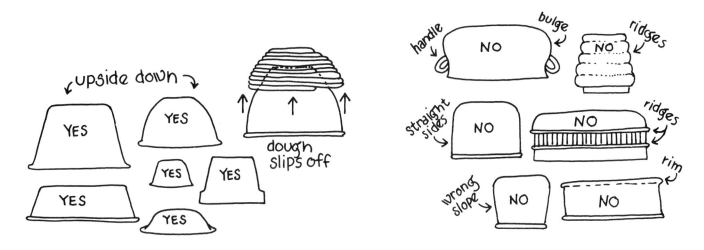

Turn the foundation upside-down and coat it with a thin film of vegetable oil (put some oil on your palms and rub them over the foundation). Roll a piece of dough into a ¼″-diameter strand as explained in No. 1. Roll only one strand at a time. Start at the center of the bottom of the bowl and begin spiraling the strand, brushing it with water as you wind so that it adheres to itself. Continue winding, adding new strands as each one is used up, joining the ends of the strands with water and smoothing the joints.

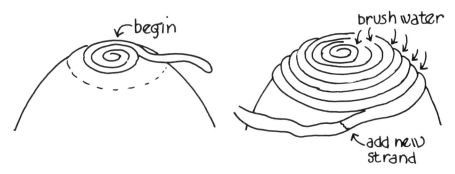

4. Cut the dough into strips and weave the strips over or inside an ovenproof foundation. (*Examples:* Planter Basket, page 42; Pie Plate Basket, page 54.)

The foundation must be so shaped that the baked dough can be slipped off easily. Baking dishes with slanted sides are excellent for the purpose.

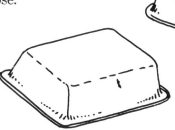

Prepare the foundation by turning it upside-down and coating it with a thin film of oil, or leaving it right side up and coating the inside with a thin film of oil.

Pat a large piece of dough into a rectangle on a floured surface. (The dough should be on the dry side, not at all sticky or weepy.) Roll the dough out with a rolling pin to about ¼″ thick. *Tip:* To get a perfectly uniform thickness, place a piece of ¼″ lattice on each side of the dough. Roll the dough out until the rolling pin rests on the lattice strips. The dough should then be flat and perfectly even.

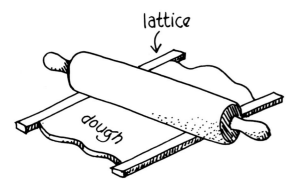

With a sharp knife, small spatula or palette knife, cut the dough into strips. The width of the strips depends on the project; you can measure with a ruler or trust your eye. The length of the strips depends on the size of the foundation you are working on. Cut about six strips at a time; wrap the dough you're not using tightly in plastic.

When working on the outside, lay the strips down on the bottom of the foundation as shown on the left. When working on the inside, lay strips on the bottom of the foundation as shown on the right. Brush water between the strips where they overlap.

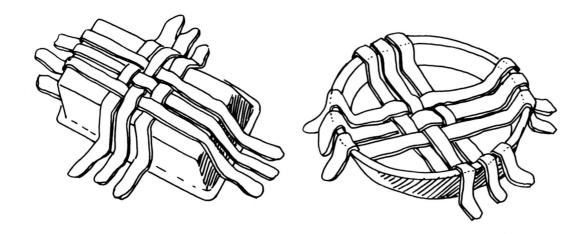

Continue rolling out dough, cutting strips and weaving them under and over until the bottom of the foundation is covered. The strips will be extending neatly along the sides of the foundation. Cut off the excess, but be sure to leave an extra inch on the end of each strip (unless the project instructions specify otherwise). The extra inch will be taken up as you weave strips around the sides.

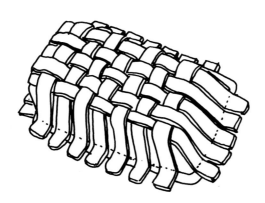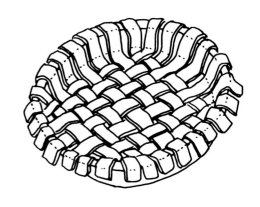

Make more strips for the sides: Join two strips, using water as glue and pressing the ends firmly together. Roll up this extra-long strip. Begin at one side of the foundation and weave this long strip around the sides, under and over, unrolling the strip as you go, until you have worked back to the beginning. (It is possible that you will have to add another piece to the strip, but try to avoid this.) Cut off any excess and join the end of the strip to the beginning, using water as glue and smoothing out the joint.

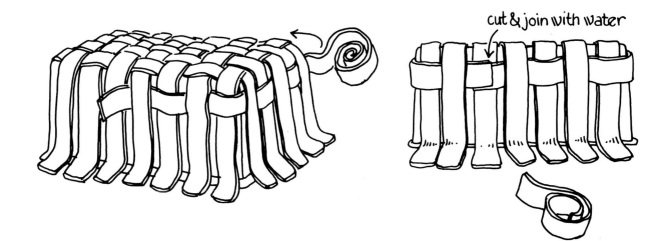

cut & join with water

Depending on the height of the sides of the foundation, you may want to add another strip around the sides, or you may want to finish off the basket in some other way.

5. Cut the dough with tiny aspic cutters or large and small cookie cutters. (*Examples:* Folk Art Star Ornament, page 79; Noel Tree, page 94.)

Dust a work surface with flour and use a rolling pin to roll out the dough to ⅛″ to ¼″ thick. Cut firmly with a cutter and transfer the shape to the back of a cookie sheet. *Tip:* Dip the cutter in a little flour before you cut the dough.

Reminder: Gather up the leftover dough, knead together and rewrap tightly.

6. Cut the dough by cutting around a pattern of thin cardboard. (*Examples:* French Horn Ornament, page 97; Pennsylvania Dutch Wall Piece, page 42.)

To make a pattern, you will need tracing paper, carbon paper and thin cardboard (shirt cardboard, oaktag or posterboard are good choices). Place the tracing paper over the full-size pattern in the book and draw the outlines with pencil. Then lay the carbon paper (inked side down) on the thin cardboard and put the tracing paper over the carbon paper. Draw firmly over the outline with pencil; the outline will transfer to the cardboard. Remove the tracing paper and carbon paper. Cut out the pattern along the outline on the cardboard.

Next, roll out the dough according to the project instructions. Lay the pattern on the dough and gently hold it in place. Cut around the pattern with a sharp-pointed kitchen knife or palette knife. Remove the pattern and set aside the excess dough. Smooth the edges of the dough if necessary. Transfer the dough shape to a flour-dusted cookie sheet.

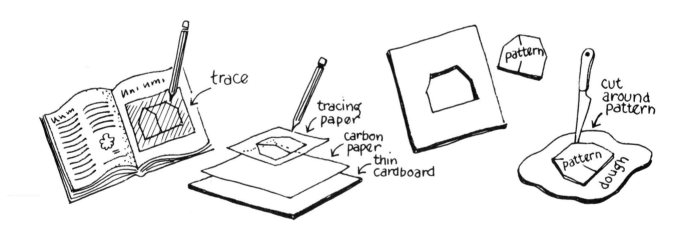

trace

tracing paper

carbon paper

thin cardboard

pattern

cut around pattern

pattern

dough

7. Use the dough in large, flat pieces with decorations layered on and cut out. (*Example:* Old MacDonald's Farm, page 150.)

Roll out the dough to ¼″ thick and transfer it to the flour-dusted back of a cookie sheet. Cut the dough following a pattern from the book, or cut around a plate or dish laid right on the dough. Add decorations to the dough or cut shapes from it.

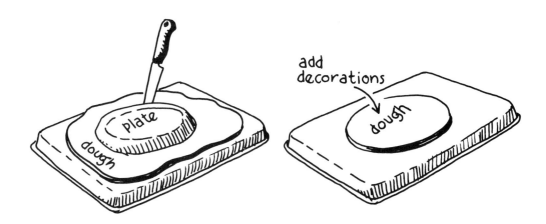

8. Shape the dough over an aluminum foil armature. (*Example:* Mexican Candleholders, page 47.)

Flour/salt dough will not hold a freestanding shape without an armature to support it. Aluminum foil can be used for this because it is light, ovenproof and—when crushed—will retain a shape. The basic principle is simple: Crush the foil and mold it to the shape you want. Cover it with pieces of dough which you overlap and smooth out. Bake the piece until it is hard and repair cracks with moist dough pressed into and smoothed over the cracks.

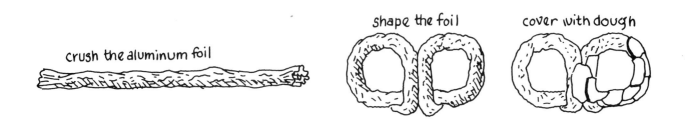

9. Model the dough by hand. (*Examples:* Berry Wreath Ornament, page 86; Turkey Place Card Holder, page 124.)

Some hand-formed pieces are simple to make, for example, the berries for the Berry Wreath are bits of dough rolled between the palms and then placed in a wreath shape, with water brushed between dough pieces to glue them together. Some hand-formed pieces are more complicated, a composite of different shapes glued together with water. Each project has specific instructions explaining how to make the shapes required to complete that particular project.

HOW TO COMBINE THE PARTS OF THE PROJECTS

There are three ways of combining the different parts of each flour/salt dough project, different for different stages: *Before baking*, the parts are glued together with water. *During baking*, additional parts may be added with a bit of water and the heat of the object to glue them together. *After baking*, use white glue or epoxy glue to put the parts together or to glue them to another surface.

Before baking: Most decorative elements are applied to dough objects *before* baking. Baking does unpredictable things to dough—the dough warps, bubbles, expands. Since you can't glue flat decorations to a puffed-out object, do your decorating before baking if possible. Before baking, water is used as a glue. You can brush it on with a paintbrush, dab it on with your finger, or even drop it on with a toothpick. Depending on the project, water should be applied either to the main piece of dough or to the back of the smaller piece that you are attaching. Use the water sparingly; excess water tends to blur the crisp lines of a piece during baking. Any spot that has been brushed with water will bake darker than the rest of the dough, so if you are working on a piece that you plan to leave natural (i.e., not painted), brush the water only where you really need it.

The three folk art Christmas ornaments shown in close-up on page 79 include good examples of decorations applied before baking. The little flowers and leaves were cut out, brushed with water on the back and placed in position on each ornament. The ornaments were then baked and painted. The Noel Tree on page 94 was done the same way: all the hearts, stars and letters were applied with water to the tree-shaped base, the whole unit baked together and later painted.

During baking: This technique is handy for two purposes. First, it's good for decorating a part of an object that is unreachable during initial baking. For example, the Bread Basket on page 64 was baked upside-down on its foundation until it was hard enough to remove from the foundation. Then it was taken out of the oven, turned right side up and decorated on the top edge—previously unreachable—with little balls. Finally, it was put back in the oven to finish baking. With this method, the decorations must be applied while the object is still very warm; it is helpful to dab on a bit of water as well.

After baking: If decorations cannot be attached in their correct positions before or during baking, you will need to glue them in place after baking both the object and the decorations. The Mexican Candleholders on page 47 were baked upright in the oven, so the decorations could not be attached—they would have fallen off. The candleholders and the decorations were baked separately, painted and then glued together with epoxy. The same basic procedure was followed for the Cookie Wreath on page 119. The foundation, roses and small leaves were baked in one piece and the decorations baked separately. When all the parts were cool, they were glued together with epoxy.

Several projects involve gluing the parts of the project to some other surface—for example, the Wooden Plate Wall Piece on page 64 and the red Flower Napkin Rings on page 47. Because of epoxy's strength and permanence, it is the glue of choice for this kind of job, although in some situations white glue may suffice.

DECORATIVE TECHNIQUES

Applied shapes: This includes all the little shapes you mold or cut by hand (squares, balls, leaves, berries, etc.) or cut with small cookie cutters or aspic cutters (animals, flowers, birds, hearts, fruits, etc.). Many are attached with water before baking; some are attached to the baked object with white glue or epoxy.

Incised lines, dots, circles, etc.: Unbaked flour/salt dough holds an impression quite well if you make it deep and sharp. Use a wooden skewer (either the pointed end or the round blunt end), toothpick, plastic bottle cap, blunt knife edge or other tool and press it firmly into the dough. Be sure to do this before the surface dries out or your impression will be cracked and unclear. Don't use a very sharp knife edge; the thin line it produces will disappear in the baking.

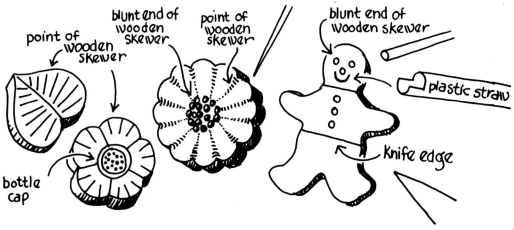

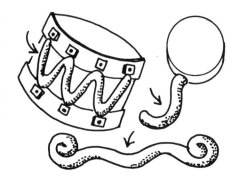

Rolled strands: Strands are rolled on a flour-dusted surface. For decorations, they may be very thin or as thick as ¼″ or more in diameter. Work quickly with strands because they dry out fast. Attach them to your unbaked dough project by brushing water on the *project*—not on the strand—and placing the strand in position on the moistened area. Neatly cut off any excess strand.

Strands can be used to make block letters, too. Roll the strand to the desired diameter, shape the letter and cut off any excess strand. Using paintbrush and water, draw the letter in the correct position on the dough project and set the pre-formed letter on the wet shape.

Garlic press strands: The fleece of the lamb and the mane of the lion on page 101 are made by forcing a piece of dough through a garlic press. Press the dough through only until the strands are the length you want. Remove a group of strands by drawing a sharp knife along the base of the strands, or remove one strand at a time with a toothpick or wooden skewer. Brush water on the project and place the strands in position. Be sure to wash the garlic press carefully before leftover dough dries on it.

garlic press

HOW TO BAKE THE FLOUR / SALT DOUGH

Bake your projects on the back of heavy-duty cookie sheets placed on the racks of your regular (not microwave) oven. Be sure to dust the back of the cookie sheet liberally with flour before placing your dough project on it or you will have a terrible time trying to get it off. Keep a couple of spatulas and pot holders handy for removing the dough pieces when they have finished baking and have some wire racks ready to hold the baked pieces while they cool.

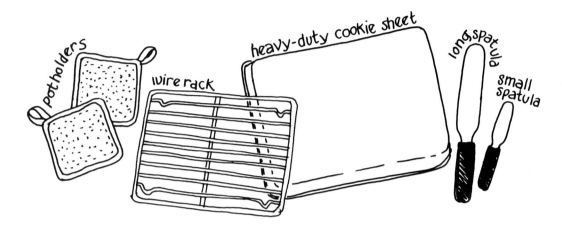

Baking is done at low heat, about 250° to 300°. The low heat keeps the dough from browning, which is desirable when you are planning to paint the piece or when you want a pale dough color, as on the Scalloped Basket, page 47. There are instances, however, when you want the dough to turn a rich brown—for example, on parts of the Cookie Wreath on page 119. All the parts of the Cookie Wreath were first baked at low heat until they were hard. The larger flowers and leaves were then returned to the oven at higher heat to brown further. You must check the dough at least every 10 minutes when the oven is set at a higher heat because it can brown significantly in a very short time.

The amount of time needed for baking runs from half an hour to several hours, varying from oven to oven and project to project. The instruction to "bake until hard" means that you must judge when the item is completely baked. Start by baking the piece for about 20 minutes and then examine it. Small items may indeed be baked thoroughly in that short a time. Larger items will need more time in the oven. You must check the dough every 20 minutes on small items and every 30 minutes on large pieces. Use your kitchen timer to remind you.

The only sure way to judge hardness is to let the item cool slightly and then press it gently as you would a cake. If it gives, it's not cooked enough. If it doesn't yield to pressure, it is probably completely baked, but you must turn it over carefully and check the underside as well. If the underside is not firm, return the object to the oven, underside up, and let it bake some more. Large dough projects (like Old MacDonald's Farm, page 150) must be left right side up in the oven for as long as it takes to bake them to hardness. *Do not try to turn them over* to allow the underside to bake.

Woven pieces, like the Pie Plate Basket on page 54, are constructed over foundations (pie plate, loaf pan, bowl, etc.) and are baked on their foundations until they are quite hard. Then they must be lifted gently from their foundations and set on the bare oven rack to continue baking, so the heat will reach the inside.

Other special cases include layered pieces, in which the dough must bake thoroughly through all the layers, and chubby pieces, in which extra time is needed to bake through all that dough.

PROBLEMS IN BAKING

It is important to distinguish between real disaster and the ordinary, characteristic imperfections of this kind of dough. The dough *will* puff, crack, split and/or warp in minor ways, so you must expect and accept this. And you may be able to repair the dough: If you see a crack or split developing during baking, you can take the piece out of the oven and try patching the crack with some moist dough. This is a bit tricky, because the hot dough quickly cooks the new, moist dough you are trying to push into the crack. Use this trick only on a piece that is going to be painted.

The only real disasters that occur in baking are when the dough splits completely apart, when the parts of a project split apart or when the project warps so badly that it is unusable. These things do happen. It may be that you have not kneaded the dough enough, or you may not have attached the parts securely enough. More likely, the dough is just behaving unpredictably and there's nothing you can do about it except throw the piece out and start again.

REPAIRING BAKED FINISHED PROJECTS

No matter how much care you give your projects, you may have to repair broken-off decorations, cracks that appear mysteriously weeks after the piece is finished, projects that have split cleanly in half, and so on.

If breakage occurs after the baking but *before* the painting, you're in luck. Glue the pieces together carefully with epoxy (or with white glue if the project is small and light), allow the glue to dry thoroughly, then paint over the break. Give it an extra coat or two of paint to cover the break completely.

If a crack appears after baking but before painting, you're in good shape too. Fill the crack neatly with spackle or caulking or even white acrylic paint. Let the filler dry completely and paint over the mended crack.

If a small painted and finished project—especially a Christmas ornament—breaks into pieces, you may very well be able to put the bits together with white glue. If a large finished project smashes to bits, throw it out and make a new one. However, if a large finished piece cracks cleanly in two or three parts, it may be worth the time and effort to put it back together neatly with epoxy glue.

HOW TO PAINT THE DOUGH

Unlike some of the other craft doughs, flour/salt dough does not mix very advantageously with food coloring. The beige tone of the unbaked dough tends to turn the food coloring muddy. The best approach is to paint the dough after it has been baked, rather than try to color it before baking.

The paints I like best are acrylics, which come in tubes and can be bought at any art supply store. They are thinned with water but are not water-soluble after they dry. Six or eight colors plus white will give you a wonderful selection which you can mix to make even more colors. A versatile group of basics would include Cadmium Red Medium, Cadmium Yellow Medium, Ultramarine Blue, Permanent Green Light, Acra Violet, Cobalt Blue and Titanium White. For greater variety, add Burnt Sienna, Permanent Green Deep, Acra Red, Dioxazine Purple and Yellow Oxide. Acrylics also come in metallic gold and silver.

Before you apply color to any dough object, paint it white (front and back) and allow the white paint to dry thoroughly. Colors painted over white will be vibrant and glowing. In general, paint the back of the project first, let that side dry, then turn it over and paint the front. Work on waxed paper.

You will often have to paint two coats of a color to get true opacity, so when you mix up a color (as opposed to using the color straight from the tube), mix enough to cover the area twice. The paints are very easy to work with but they do dry quickly—an advantage when you are waiting to paint on another coat or color but a disadvantage if you want to save some carefully mixed paint. Work with them accordingly.

You will need good-quality brushes for painting. Don't waste your money on cheap brushes that will shed their hair, make streaky strokes and ruin your work. It's far better to invest in three medium-priced brushes that will enhance your work and feel good in your hand. Buy one small pointed brush, one larger pointed brush and a wide, flat brush for covering large areas. Ask the art supply salesperson to help you choose. These brushes, especially the wide one, will serve for polyurethaning your work, too, if you clean and maintain them properly.

Take care of your brushes this way: Rinse them well in lots of clean water as you work. When you have finished working with the brushes, rinse them under cold running water, lather them gently with ordinary hand soap and then rinse the soap out thoroughly. Smooth the bristles into shape. Store brushes in a jar, handle down, so the bristles dry in the air.

Buy yourself a pad of disposable palettes to complete your painting kit. The disposable palettes are pieces of well-waxed white paper which you throw away at the end of a painting session.

Remember that acrylic paints are thinned with water. Squeeze some paint from the tube (a little goes a long way) onto the palette paper. Take your brush and mix in a few drops of water, enough to give the paint a consistency like heavy cream. Mix until the diluted paint is blended and smooth.

FINISHING THE FLOUR / SALT DOUGH PROJECTS

After the piece has been baked, you must finish it on the front *and* back with several layers of hard, protective coating.

Unpainted pieces, like the Scalloped Basket on page 47 and the Cookie Wreath on page 119, are brushed first with a coat of sealer, a half-and-half mixture of turpentine and good-quality, satin-finish polyurethane stirred together in a small jar. Brush the sealer on one side of the project and set the piece aside to dry on waxed paper. When it is dry, turn it over and paint the other side. Let this coat dry thoroughly. Brush on two, three or four coats of polyurethane, allowing each coat to dry before applying the next. The process may take several days.

Painted pieces are brushed with three or four coats of pure polyurethane. Brush one side of the piece and set it aside to dry on waxed paper. When that side is dry, turn the piece over and polyurethane the other side. Repeat this process two or three more times, letting each coat dry before applying the next.

Brushes used to apply polyurethane should be cleaned first in turpentine and then with cold water and ordinary hand soap. Be sure you get all the polyurethane out of the brushes or they will stiffen up and be unusable.

BREAD/GLUE DOUGH

The vegetables on the memo board on page 54, the miniature furniture and foods on page 155 and the jewelry on pages 160 and 164 are all made of a remarkable dough I call bread/glue dough. It is made from day-old white bread and white glue kneaded together to make a baby-smooth mixture that needs no baking, holds delicate shapes with ease and has a fine-grained finish. The dough is inedible, of course, so don't let the kids snack on it. However, it is very sturdy when dry so the completed projects can stand up to children's handling.

The dough should be tinted before you work with it because its natural color is uninteresting. Ordinary food coloring tints this dough beautifully, giving you a range of colors from pale pastels to quite intense hues. Bread/glue dough can be rolled out and cut with cookie cutters or a sharp knife or it can be modeled by hand. A modest amount goes a long way because this dough is most suitable for small items. If you wrap leftovers very tightly in plastic and keep them in an airtight container or plastic bag in the refrigerator, the dough will last for weeks.

Ingredients:

   8 slices of day-old white bread
      (the less-expensive, fluffy type)
   ½ cup white glue

Cut the crusts off the bread and tear the bread into little pieces. Put the pieces in a bowl and pour the glue over them. Use one hand to mix the bread and glue together into a sticky, well-blended mass. Gather the mass into a ball and take it out of the bowl. With both hands, pat the sticky ball of dough into a neater ball and keep patting until it is just tacky. Dust a working surface with flour and begin to knead the dough gently. As it becomes smoother and more pliable, knead it firmly. Continue to knead until the dough is satiny, about 5 minutes. Wrap the dough tightly in plastic.

Reminder: Always keep whatever dough you're not using wrapped tightly and store the dough in the refrigerator when you have finished using it for the day.

HOW TO COLOR THE DOUGH

Use ordinary food coloring to tint the dough. Break off a finger of dough and flatten it out. Sprinkle a few drops of food coloring on the dough piece and roll it up. Knead with your fingers until the color is evenly dispersed. If the dough becomes very sticky, dust it with a little flour. Rewrap tightly.

   You will have to experiment with the colors to be able to predict how the color will dry. Here are some guidelines:
1. Pink, lavender, peach, orange, yellow-green and yellow will dry darker than the moist dough appears.
2. Blue or green (with no yellow added) will dry lighter than the moist dough appears.
3. Whether used singly or in combination, food colorings can yield either a pastel or an intense color, depending on how many drops you work into the dough. Varying quantities of yellow coloring will give light yellow or bright yellow; red plus blue will give you lavender or purple; red will give light pink or dark pink; yellow plus red will give peach or orange; yellow plus green will give you light yellow-green or bright grass green.

BASIC EQUIPMENT FOR
BREAD / GLUE DOUGH PROJECTS

These are the items needed most often. Other materials necessary for specific projects are indicated at the beginning of each project.

Food coloring	*Sharp knife*
Rolling pin	*Ruler*
Cookie cutters, large and small,	*Wooden skewers, toothpicks*
depending on the project	*White glue*
Aspic cutters, depending on the project	*Waxed paper*

TWO BASIC TECHNIQUES FOR
SHAPING BREAD / GLUE DOUGH

1. Cut the dough with large or small cookie cutters or with tiny aspic cutters. (*Example:* Pink Pig Pin, page 164.)

Dust a surface with flour and roll out the dough with a rolling pin to ⅛" thick. Cut firmly with the cutter and use a spatula to transfer the shape to waxed paper to dry. Rough edges can be smoothed with a moistened finger or paintbrush. Gather up leftovers immediately, knead them together (adding a drop or two of water if necessary) and rewrap tightly.

2. Model the dough by hand. (*Examples:* vegetables on the Kitchen Memo Board, page 54; Hearts-and-Beads Necklace, page 160.)

Some hand-modeled shapes are very simple to make: A bead is a bit of dough rolled to a sphere between your palms and pierced with a small nail. Some shapes are a bit more complicated. A pea pod is a flattened oval pinched up at the ends and filled with tiny green spheres.

Each project has individual instructions explaining how to make the shapes required for completing the project.

HOW TO WORK WITH BREAD / GLUE DOUGH

This dough tends to lose moisture and stiffen up if it is exposed to the air for any length of time, so knead a few drops of water into it now and then as you work. If you overdo the water and the dough gets sticky, knead in a little flour. As long as you correct the dryness or stickiness, the dough can be worked and reworked as much as you like. Keep all dough tightly wrapped in plastic when you are not using it.

After you cut or model each shape, transfer it to waxed paper to dry. The dough is air-dried but you must turn the pieces every few hours so that they dry evenly. Tiny pieces dry quickly but large, flat pieces and thick pieces may take overnight or even a couple of days. Be sure to allow the dough to dry thoroughly before you proceed with your project. You can leave the dough pieces in an unlit oven overnight to speed the drying process.

While the dough is still moist, pieces can be glued together using water applied with a paintbrush or finger. Apply the water sparingly and press the dough pieces together firmly. Once the dough is dry, use white glue to put pieces together or to attach them to something like the Kitchen Memo Board.

The air-dried dough has a matte finish which I happen to like, so I prefer not to apply a sealer. If you do want to seal the work to give it a longer life or a slight sheen, brush on several coats of satin-finish polyurethane, allowing each coat to dry before applying the next. *Reminder:* After use, clean the brush first in turpentine and then with cold water and ordinary hand soap. Be sure to get all the polyurethane out of the brush.

SUGAR PASTE DOUGH

Take a look at the Christmas ornaments on pages 105 to 107, the vase on page 74 and the Valentine boxes on page 137. They are made of sugar paste dough, a blend of gelatin, confectioner's sugar and water. Simply mix the ingredients according to the recipe to form a ball of dough and knead it to a satiny smoothness. The dough is then tinted with food coloring and worked in a number of ways: It can be coiled, rolled flat and cut, shaped by hand or molded over small jars.

My approach to sugar paste is first to make a basic object—vase, box, basket or ornament—and set it aside to dry. Then I make little decorations for the object and set them aside to dry. When all the parts are completely dry, I glue the decorations to the object and let the glue dry. You might like to start by making the simple Christmas ornaments and Easter eggs and work your way up to the more elaborate sugar paste projects.

As you can see in the photographs, projects made of sugar paste dough are exquisitely delicate and dainty. What you may not be able to see is that they are also extremely fragile. You must handle them very carefully. When you store the pieces, wrap them in layers and layers of tissue paper and put them safely away in plastic boxes.

Reminder: Although the ingredients of sugar paste dough are harmless, the objects you make are *not* meant to be eaten.

Ingredients:

> 1½ teaspoons unflavored gelatin
> ¼ cup cold water
> 1 pound confectioner's sugar
> Cornstarch

Sprinkle the gelatin over ¼ cup cold water in a small heatproof container. Let it stand for 5 minutes. Place the container in a pan of hot water and heat gently, stirring to dissolve the gelatin. Remove from the heat and pour into a mixing bowl. Add the confectioner's sugar a little at a time, mixing after each addition. Gather the dough into a ball and knead it on a cornstarch-dusted surface unil the dough is satiny. If the dough is too stiff to knead, add a few drops of water. If the dough is too sticky, dust it with a little cornstarch. Wrap immediately in plastic wrap. The dough can be stored in the refrigerator for several days.

HOW TO COLOR THE DOUGH

Use ordinary food coloring to tint the dough. Pinch off a finger of dough and flatten it out. Sprinkle a few drops of food coloring on the piece of dough and roll it up. Knead until the color is evenly dispersed. If the dough becomes too sticky, dust it with cornstarch. Rewrap tightly in a piece of plastic wrap. Repeat this process to make as many colors as you like. *Note:*

Colors dry lighter so compensate by coloring the moist dough a little more intensely than you actually want it to be.

Reminder: Red food coloring makes light pink or dark pink; blue makes light blue; green makes light green; green plus yellow makes grass green; red plus blue makes lavender; yellow makes light yellow; yellow plus red makes peach or orange; uncolored dough dries bright white.

BASIC EQUIPMENT FOR SUGAR PASTE DOUGH PROJECTS

These are the items needed most often. Other materials necessary for specific projects are indicated at the beginning of each project.

Food coloring
Rolling pin
Sharp knife
Pastry cutter
Paintbrush
Small and large spatulas

Tweezers
Toothpicks
White glue
Cookie cutters, large and small,
* depending on the project*
Aspic cutters, depending on the project

FIVE BASIC TECHNIQUES FOR SHAPING SUGAR PASTE DOUGH

1. Cut the dough with large or small cookie cutters or with tiny aspic cutters. (*Examples:* Ruffled Fan Ornament, page 105; Petals-and-Pearls Ornament, page 107.)

Dust a surface with cornstarch and roll out the dough with a rolling pin to 1/16″ to 1/8″ thick. Cut firmly with cutter and use a small spatula to transfer the shape to waxed paper to dry. Gather up leftovers immediately, knead them together (adding a drop or two of water if necessary) and rewrap.

2. Mold the dough over a foundation (a small jar, plastic container or metal box). (*Examples:* Valentine Basket with Roses, page 137; Flower-Topped Box, page 142.)

Roll out the dough and cut it either with a large cookie cutter or in a basic box shape. Place the cut dough over a jar or other foundation turned upside-down. Join the corners with water if necessary. Allow to dry completely before removing from the foundation.

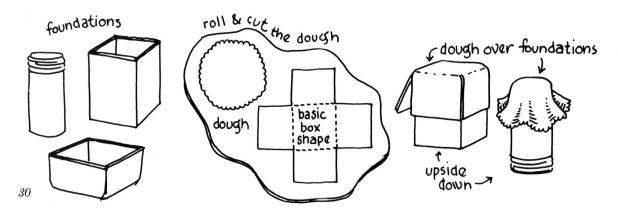

Note: The foundation you use must have no protruding ridge or lip around the bottom. If it did, it would be impossible to remove the dry dough without breaking it.

3. Mold the dough around a cookie cutter. (*Examples:* Heart-Shaped Box, page 137; Easter Basket, page 142.)

Roll out the dough and cut strips of dough to fit around the cookie cutter. Join the strips by painting the ends with water and pinching them together. Allow this molded section to dry and then remove the cutter. The bottom of the box is cut separately and allowed to dry. The molded section is glued to the bottom to form the sides of the completed box.

4. Roll the dough into strands and coil it around a straight-sided jar. (*Example:* Sugar Paste Vase, page 74.)

Break off a finger-sized piece of dough and roll it into a strand about ³⁄₁₆″ to ¼″ in diameter. Working quickly, begin to coil it around the jar, starting at the bottom of the jar. Brush the top of the strand with water as you coil so the strand will adhere to itself. With a sharp knife, cut the end of the strand at a steep diagonal. Roll another strand, cut the beginning of the new strand at a complementary steep diagonal and join it to the first strand with a bit of water. Smooth the two strands together and continue coiling around the jar.

Continue adding strands in this fashion as needed until the jar is covered with coiled strands.

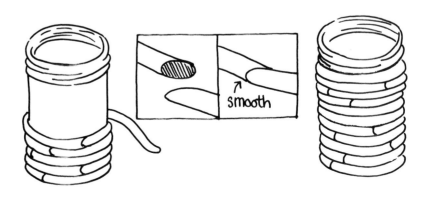

5. Form small decorations by molding them by hand.(*Examples:* flower on the lid of the Flower-Topped Box on page 142; flowers and some of the decorations on the Heart-Shaped Box on page 137, and some of the decorations on the Sugar Paste Vase on page 74.)

Decorations are shown on page 33. The general idea is to break off small bits of dough and roll them between your fingers to form balls, petals, ovals and other shapes.

HOW TO WORK WITH SUGAR PASTE DOUGH

The most important thing to remember when working with sugar paste dough is that it *dries* very quickly when exposed to air, so you must *work* quickly when shaping the dough. This is especially crucial when you are rolling strands for coiled vases or shaping any of the boxes. If a piece of dough seems to be surface-drying and cracking unattractively, simply crumple it up, dab it with a few drops of water and knead it back to smoothness.

Any time the dough you're working with seems to be too stiff and dry, wet your fingers and knead the moisture back into the dough. Keep all dough wrapped tightly in plastic when you are not using it. While the dough is still moist, rough edges can be smoothed gently with a wet finger or paintbrush.

All decorations should be transferred carefully to waxed paper to dry. Cookie cutter shapes can be moved with a large or small spatula. All boxes and baskets should be constructed directly on waxed paper.

Small, flat pieces like birds and hearts should be turned over every hour or two so they dry evenly. Small three-dimensional pieces like roses should be allowed to harden for a couple of hours before being turned over. Larger three-dimensional pieces like boxes and baskets must be allowed to dry almost completely (perhaps overnight) before you can risk turning them over or removing them from their foundations. Hand-formed decorative pieces like balls and petals dry quickly and need only occasional turning.

Before it dries, dough can be glued with water. For example, adjacent edges of a box can be joined by brushing them with water, pinching them together and smoothing them down with a bit more water. The petals of a rose are layered with water brushed on to act as glue.

After dough is dry, use white glue to put elements together. Decorations are applied by lifting them with tweezers, dipping them into glue and then placing them in position on the sugar paste object. You can also dab glue directly onto the sugar paste object with a toothpick, then use the tweezers to set the decoration in place on the glue. When you are gluing decorations in layers, be sure to allow the glue to dry completely on one layer before applying the next.

Use white glue when replacing decorations that break or fall off. Large clean breaks in a sugar paste object can sometimes be repaired by applying white glue neatly and sparingly to the break and pressing the pieces back together. White glue is also used to add lace, gold trim, pearls, beads and colored candies to the sugar paste objects.

DECORATIONS FOR SUGAR PASTE PROJECTS

The drawings below show a variety of decorations you can make to glue to
your sugar paste objects.

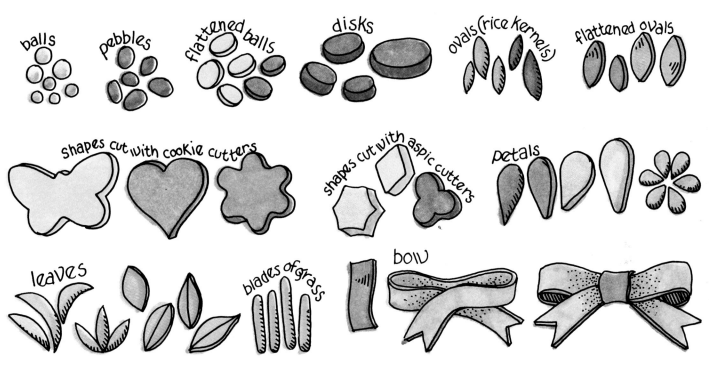

HOW TO MAKE ROSEBUDS AND ROSES

A rosebud is simply a sphere of dough flattened into an oval, painted with
water along the lower edge and rolled up.

A rose starts with a rosebud. Add one or two oval petals around the bud,
brushing the lower edge of each petal with water and overlapping it on the
previous petal. Open out the petals slightly. If the rose is going to sit on a
flat surface (like the Heart-Shaped Box), you must carefully cut off the
pointed end with a sharp knife.

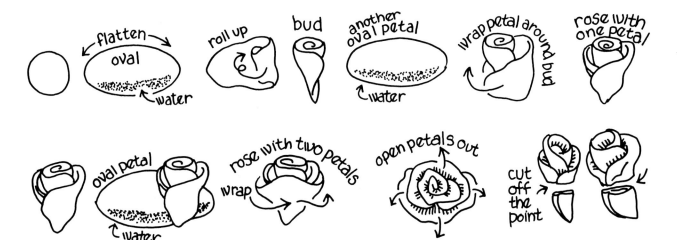

NOTES ON GLUE

WHITE GLUE This is an all-purpose, thick, white liquid glue that dries clear. It is durable, easy to work with, waterproof and long-lasting but not permanent. There are many brands of white glue; I prefer Sobo or Elmer's Glue. Look for it in a squeezable plastic container with a pointed tip. It's available in the five-and-ten, hardware store, supermarket, stationery store and art supply store.

EPOXY GLUE Use epoxy when you need a really strong, permanent bond. It is a two-part glue (each part comes in its own container) and must be mixed as you need it. Squeeze equal amounts of each part onto waxed paper, mix them thoroughly with a toothpick and apply the glue with the toothpick. I prefer the 5-minute type, which will hold a decoration in place in less than 5 minutes. Let the glue dry overnight to get the full benefit of the permanent bond. Epoxy is available in the five-and-ten and in hardware stores.

GINGERBREAD DOUGH

The Gingerbread Folks on page 116 and the Gingerbread House on pages 104 and 110 are made with this deliciously edible dough.

Ingredients:

> 1 cup (2 sticks) margarine
> 1 packed cup brown sugar
> 1 tablespoon cinnamon
> 1 tablespoon ginger
> 1 cup dark corn syrup
> 2 eggs
> 1½ teaspoons baking soda
> 5½ cups flour

Cream the margarine, sugar and spices together until fluffy. Add the corn syrup and eggs and beat until thoroughly blended. Mix the baking soda into the flour and add to the creamed mixture. Blend until you have a ball of smooth dough. Remove from the bowl and wrap tightly in plastic wrap. Chill the dough overnight.

When you are ready to roll out the dough, first dust your surface with flour. Roll the dough to ⅛″ to ¼″ thick and cut the cookies or parts of the Gingerbread House. Transfer them to the ungreased *back* of a heavy-duty cookie sheet for baking, leaving plenty of space between the cookies—they expand during baking. Bake in a preheated 375° oven. Cookies and small pieces require 7 to 10 minutes of baking; watch them carefully. Bake large pieces 12 to 15 minutes.

Use a long spatula to loosen the cookies from the cookie sheet while the cookies are still very warm. Remove them carefully and place on wire racks to cool completely.

COOKIE DOUGH

This is a basic cookie recipe I use for Valentine Cookies, page 130, and Christmas Cookies, page 91. Because they are not overly sweet, these cookies are the perfect foil for icing decorations.

Ingredients:

    ½ cup sugar
    ½ cup (1 stick) margarine
    2 eggs
    1 teaspoon vanilla
  2½ cups flour
    2 teaspoons baking powder

Cream sugar and margarine until fluffy. Add eggs and vanilla and beat well. Add flour and baking powder; mix to form a ball of dough. Wrap the dough in plastic and refrigerate for several hours. When you are ready to roll out the dough, dust your surface with flour, roll the dough to ⅛″ thick and cut out the cookies. Use a spatula to transfer the cookies to the ungreased back of a cookie sheet, leaving 1″ between cookies. Bake in a preheated 375° oven for 8 to 12 minutes. Remove the baked cookies from the cookie sheet almost immediately, before they have a chance to cool and stick to the cookie sheet. Let the cookies cool on wire racks.

NOTES ON COOKIE CUTTERS

Cookie cutters are used frequently in this book. I'm sure you already have at least a few basics—plain round, scalloped round, doughnut shape, heart, Christmas tree, bell.

If you don't have every cutter you need for a particular project, borrow the necessary cutters from a neighbor or invest in some new ones. Any good housewares department will have a selection of individual cutters, but you should also consider buying *sets* of canapé cutters, aspic cutters and

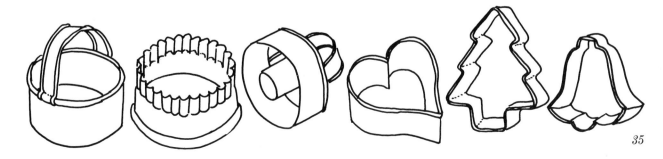

small cookie cutters. For example, you could buy a set of tiny animal cutters, a set of nested hearts in graduated sizes, a set of four flower shapes in two different sizes or a set of Christmas theme cookie cutters.

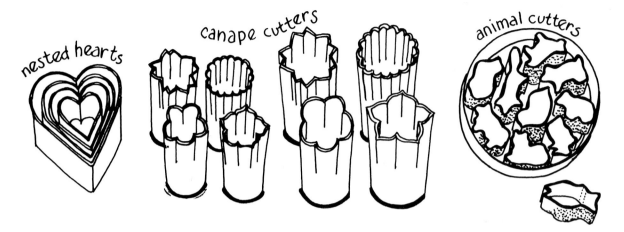

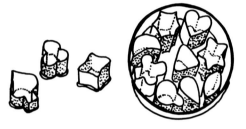

If you can only afford one set, buy tiny aspic cutters that come in a round tin and include a heart, diamond, five-pointed star, six-pointed star, crescent, triangle, leaf and several other shapes.

Feel free to substitute one cookie cutter for another as long as a substitution will not affect the construction of the piece. For instance, on the Noel Tree (page 94) you could not use large stars in place of the scalloped rounds that make up the basic tree: the large stars would not provide a sturdy foundation for the decorations. But on that same Noel Tree you could change the small stars to flowers and the small hearts to bells.

Very often the size of a project can be changed, as long as you alter the decorations correspondingly. For example, you could use a 2½″ or 3½″ scalloped round for the Round Ruffled Ornament (page 106) instead of the 3″ round specified in the instructions, provided you made the roses proportionately smaller or larger.

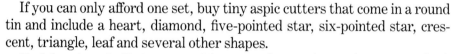

DECORATING ICING

Even if you have never piped icing decorations before, you'll find this icing very easy to work with. It takes the food coloring beautifully and dries hard and crisp. This icing is used on all the cookies and gingerbread that are included in the book.

Ingredients:

    1 pound confectioner's sugar
    3 egg whites
    ¾ teaspoon cream of tartar

Mix all the ingredients in a deep bowl. Beat at high speed for 5 minutes. Keep the icing covered tightly with plastic wrap until ready to use it.

HOW TO COLOR THE ICING

Divide the icing into separate small bowls—as many bowls as you want colors. (You'll want to leave the icing in one bowl white.) Cover each bowl tightly with plastic wrap. Remove the wrap to do the coloring and then cover tightly again. Add a few drops of ordinary food coloring to each bowl. The more coloring you use, the darker the color, but don't use so much that the icing becomes diluted. Use a small spatula or knife to stir the coloring vigorously into the icing.

PASTRY BAGS AND ICING TIPS

The decorating icing is applied to the cookies using a pastry bag and icing tips. Don't be misled by the term "pastry bag"—that's what you ask for at the store but it's used for icing as well as pastry. I like the 10″ bags made of plastic-lined muslin but you might prefer those made of plastic. Any good housewares store or housewares department should have them. They will also have the icing tips you need. There are dozens of sizes and shapes of icing tips for making all kinds of borders, flowers and leaves but for my cookies you will only need a small round tip (Ateco brand, #2, about 1/16″ in diameter) and a small star tip (Wilton brand, #27, about 3/16″ in diameter).

When you buy the pastry bags, be sure to buy a coupler for each bag. The coupler consists of two plastic parts: a sort of threaded nozzle which is inserted into the pastry bag before you fill the bag with icing, and a threaded ring that fits over the icing tip and secures the tip to the pastry bag and nozzle.

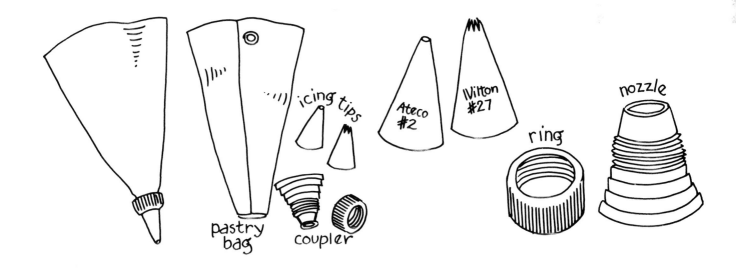

If you can afford it, buy several pastry bags (one for each color you plan to use for decorating) and several of each tip. Remember to buy one coupler for each pastry bag. You can, of course, make do with just one bag, one coupler and two tips but decorating will be easier and more fun if you can have several colors ready to go in several bags.

ASSEMBLING AND FILLING THE PASTRY BAG

The narrow end of the pastry bag will first have to be cut down to allow the nozzle of the coupler to slip through it. Insert the nozzle into the narrow end of the pastry bag and estimate how much to cut off to allow about three rounds of threading to fit through. Take the nozzle out and cut off the end of the bag. Reinsert the nozzle and see if you have cut off enough. Cut off more if necessary, and then push the nozzle firmly into place in the pastry bag. Now place the icing tip over the nozzle and slip the threaded ring over the tip. Screw the ring on securely.

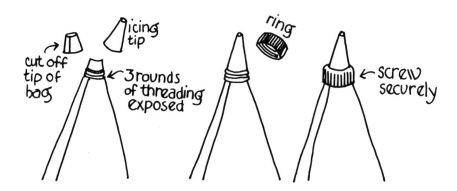

To fill the bag with icing, first fold the bag down to form a cuff while holding the bag open in your hand. Use a small spatula or knife to put the icing in; fill the bag only half full. Fold the cuff back up and fold the sides of the bag over as shown in the drawing. Roll the end down and grasp the folded end with one hand. With your other hand you will press out the icing and guide the flow from the tip.

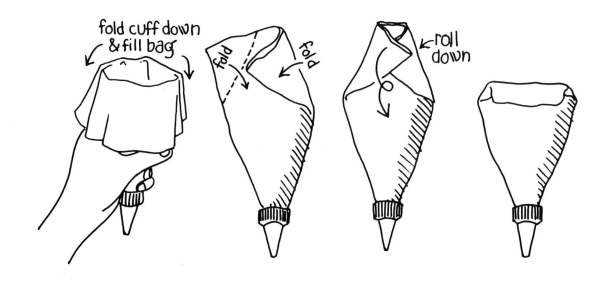

38

HOW TO PIPE LINES, DOTS, LOOPS AND STARS

Now you can begin to practice on waxed paper with your filled pastry bag and round tip. Start by trying a few lines: Hold the bag at about a 30° angle from the paper and squeeze out the icing continuously and smoothly as you move your hand to make the line. Do this until you feel confident. The tip should just touch the surface of the paper (or cookie). Don't dig in or drag the tip. Don't worry about getting a perfectly straight line—your designs will be pretty even if your lines are wiggly. Aim for feeling comfortable with your equipment rather than achieving perfection.

Next try some dots: With the round tip, hold the bag perpendicular to the paper with the tip barely touching the surface. Squeeze out a little bit of icing and, as the icing forms a tiny mound, lift the tip, stop squeezing and move the tip away. Go on to the next dot. The same technique is used for piping tiny stars with the star tip.

Loops are made the same way as lines, but you simply guide the round tip in a scallop pattern. Loops can be large or small and they certainly don't have to be perfectly regular. Make them as regular as you can without measuring or worrying. Curlicues are close kin to loops so try a few of those, too. And just for good measure, pipe a few bows with the round tip, then switch to the star tip and pipe a few more bows. By now you should be confident enough to work on a real cookie.

At this point there is nothing else you need to know about piping. When you get to the cookie and gingerbread projects, you will find diagrams that clearly delineate the designs and show you which tips to use on each part of a design.

Note: This icing is also used as a glue when you are layering cookie shapes or parts of the Gingerbread House. Simply pipe a small amount of white icing on the back of the piece to be glued and press it into position.

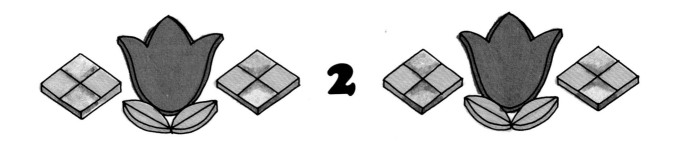

Baskets, Bowls, Centerpieces and Wall Pieces

We get the most craft satisfaction from making things that are as useful as they are beautiful. This is a chapter of accessories that will enhance your kitchen, dining room and living room. Please note the photograph on page 69, which gives you a different and helpful view of the baskets and bowls.

Important: Before you begin any project, take time to check the "You will need" list to find out what kind of dough is required. Then turn back to Chapter 1 and read all the general information on that kind of dough so you'll know exactly what you're doing.

Pennsylvania Dutch Wall Piece, page 43
Planter Basket, page 45

Pennsylvania Dutch Wall Piece

You will need:

1 recipe of flour/salt dough

Tracing paper, carbon paper and thin cardboard for making patterns

Rolling pin

Cookie cutters: small flower, about 1½″ across; small heart, about 1¼″ across

Sharp knife; wooden skewer or toothpick

Cookie sheet

Acrylic paints, brushes

Polyurethane, turpentine

Wood frame, with window 7½″ x 9½″ and wide, flat molding

Piece of linen or synthetic linen, 10″ x 12″, to cover cardboard backing

Piece of linen or synthetic linen, 7¾″ x 9¾″, to cover back of cardboard

Piece of white felt, 7½″ x 9½″

Epoxy glue, white glue

Photograph, page 42, for design and color guidance

Note: Read the general information about flour/salt dough in Chapter 1, giving special attention to Technique #6 on page 18.

MAKING THE DOUGH PIECES

Transfer and cut out the patterns (see how-to on page 18). Roll out the dough to ⅛″ to ¼″ thick. Place patterns on dough and use a sharp knife to cut out one tulip head, two small diamonds, two large diamonds, two upper

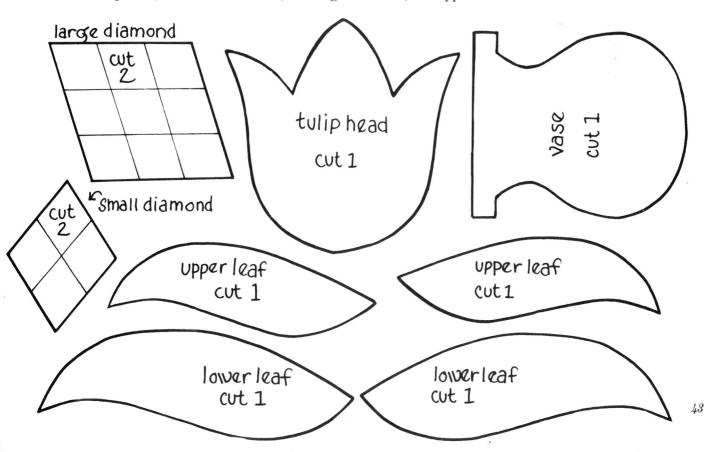

large diamond
cut 2

small diamond
cut 2

tulip head
cut 1

vase
cut 1

upper leaf
cut 1

upper leaf
cut 1

lower leaf
cut 1

lower leaf
cut 1

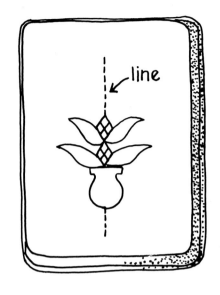

leaves, two lower leaves and one vase. Use the cookie cutters to cut out nine small hearts and two flowers. Form by hand four tiny tulip heads and eight tiny leaves that will fit on the flat molding of the frame (see photograph, page 42).

Tip: Cut a few extra hearts and flowers and form a few extra tiny tulip heads and leaves. After baking, you can choose the best of the crop for your finished piece.

Incise the lines on the diamonds with the blunt edge of the knife according to the indications on the pattern. Incise the circle and lines on the flowers, using a little round cap of some kind and a wooden skewer or toothpick.

BAKING THE DOUGH PIECES

With marking pen or grease pencil, draw a line down the middle of the back of the cookie sheet. Dust the cookie sheet with flour. Lay out the leaves, small diamonds and vase, using the line as a guide to center the dough pieces.

Brush water between the pieces to join them. Brush water on the vase and center a small heart on it. Roll a strand of dough about 1/8″ in diameter and 10″ long; center it under the vase and spiral the ends as in the photograph. Brush water between the strand and the vase to join them and around the spiral to keep it in position.

Transfer all other dough pieces to the back of the cookie sheet, place the sheet in the oven and bake at low heat until the pieces are hard. Do *not* turn the pieces over during baking.

Remove from the oven and allow to cool.

FINISHING THE DOUGH PIECES

First paint the pieces white. When the white paint has dried, paint on bright colors like those in the photograph or invent your own color scheme. Allow the painted pieces to dry, then brush on several coats of polyurethane, letting each coat dry thoroughly before applying the next.

PUTTING THE PIECES TOGETHER

Discard all parts of the frame except the wooden molding, the cardboard backing piece and the clips that hold the parts together. Glue the white felt to the cardboard backing piece, using only a few dabs of white glue. Iron the larger piece of linen and use white glue to fasten it around the felt-covered cardboard, as shown in the diagram. Iron the smaller piece of linen and glue it to the back of the cardboard to cover all the raw edges.

Replace the cardboard—now covered neatly with linen—in the frame and clip it in place. Turn the frame right side up and lay out the painted dough pieces on the molding and on the linen, following the photograph. Glue each piece in place with epoxy. Allow the epoxy to dry overnight.

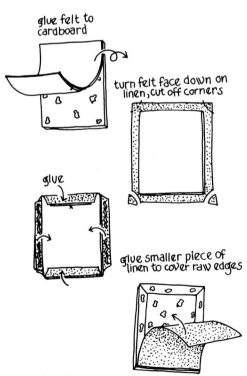

glue felt to cardboard

turn felt face down on linen, cut off corners

glue

glue smaller piece of linen to cover raw edges

Planter Basket

You will need:

1 recipe of flour/salt dough

Loaf pan, lightly oiled on the outside. (Any size loaf pan will do. Mine is 7⅜″ x 3⅝″ x 2½″, which accommodates two small plants.)

Rolling pin

Ruler, sharp knife

Acrylic paints, brushes

Polyurethane, turpentine

Photograph, page 42, for design and color guidance

Note: When you read the general information about flour/salt dough in Chapter 1, give special attention to Technique #4 on page 15. Take a close look at the photograph on page 69 to get another view of the Planter Basket.

MAKING THE DOUGH STRIPS AND WEAVING THE BOTTOM OF THE BASKET

Roll the dough out on a floured surface to ¼″ thick, in a rectangular shape. The rectangle must be at least 3″ longer than the measurement of the loaf pan from end to end.

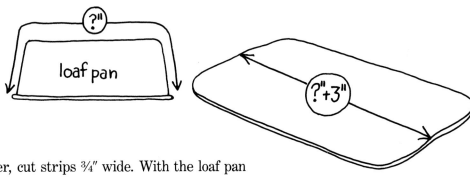

Using a sharp knife and a ruler, cut strips ¾″ wide. With the loaf pan upside-down, lay three strips lengthwise, centered and close together. Lay three more strips on the pan, perpendicular and centered, weaving them under and over. Dab water between the strips where they overlap.

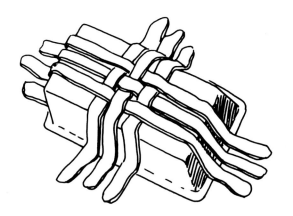

45

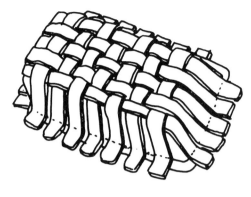

Roll out and cut more dough if necessary and continue adding strips and weaving them together until the bottom of the pan is covered with woven dough. The unwoven part of the strips should lie neatly on the sides of the pan.

WEAVING THE SIDES

Each side is woven with short strips, which are then joined at the corners of the loaf pan.

Roll dough out to ¼″ thick in a rectangle 3″ longer than the length of the loaf pan. Cut the dough in strips ¾″ wide. Weave these new strips under and over the strips on one long side of the loaf pan, dabbing water on the strips where they overlap. Space them so the final strip rests on the lip of the pan. Cut off excess strips at the edge of the lip.

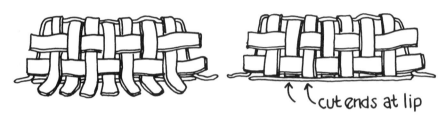

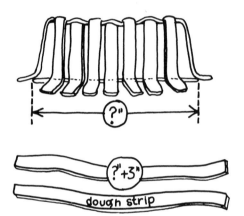

Repeat this procedure on the remaining long side and the short sides of the loaf pan, using the same number of strips on each side. Match the strips up at the corners and pinch each pair of strips together with a bit of water to join them securely. Cut off excess strips with a sharp knife.

Bake at low heat until almost completely hard. Remove the basket from the loaf pan gently and turn it right side up.

ADDING THE LEAF DECORATIONS

While the basket is still very warm, add chubby leaves around the top edge. Form each leaf by hand and incise the center line with the blunt edge of a knife. Brush the top edge of the pan with water and set one leaf in place. Place a second leaf snugly against the first leaf, brushing a bit of water between them. Work all the way around the top edge. Return the basket to the oven and bake until the leaves are hard. Remove from the oven and allow to cool.

FINISHING THE BASKET

Note: There is no white underpainting in this project.

Paint the basket with acrylic paint as shown in the photographs or invent your own color scheme. When the paint is completely dry, brush a coat of sealer (see page 26) on the whole basket.

Allow the sealer to dry thoroughly and then brush on several coats of polyurethane, allowing each coat to dry before applying the next.

Tip: Line the Planter Basket with several layers of aluminum foil or plastic wrap before putting in your potted plants.

Mexican Candleholders, page 48
Scalloped Basket, page 51
Flower Napkin Rings, page 53

Mexican Candleholder

You will need:

1 recipe of flour/salt dough
Aluminum foil
Rolling pin
Cookie cutters: small bird; flower
    with eight petals, about 2″ in
    diameter; scalloped round,
    about 1½″ in diameter; small
    crescent (optional)
Paper clips, wire cutters

Wooden skewers
Cookie sheet
Acrylic paints, brushes
Polyurethane, turpentine
Epoxy glue (the 5-minute type)

*Photograph, page 47, for design
and color guidance*

Note: Familiarize yourself with Technique #8 on page 19 of Chapter 1.

MAKING THE ARMATURE

The candleholder is constructed over an aluminum foil foundation. Tear off a 27″ length of foil and scrunch it into a long snake. Fasten the ends at the center and round out the foil arms. Wrap the center stem and the base with pieces of aluminum foil to shape them and smooth them out.

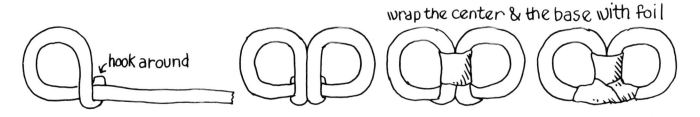

COVERING THE ARMATURE WITH DOUGH

Begin at the base and cover the armature with small pieces of dough ¼″ thick. Blend each piece into the next, smoothing and patching if necessary. Use larger pieces of dough around the arms of the candleholder. Be sure to cover every part of the armature *except* the underside of the base. Add a little bit to fill in at the top.

    With the wire cutters, clip two U-shaped pieces from the paper clips and insert them in the dough.

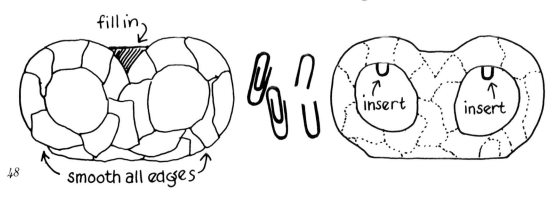

MAKING THE CANDLE RECEPTACLE AND BAKING THE CANDLEHOLDER

Roll four short strands of dough, each about 6″ long and ¼″ in diameter. Brush water on the center top of the candleholder and place one strand of dough in a ring on it. Cut off the excess strand and join the ends with water, smoothing them neatly. Brush water on the top of the strand and cover it with another ring, cutting off the excess and smoothing the ends. Repeat with the remaining two strands. The joints should all be on the same side— that will be the back of the candleholder.

Place the candleholder on a cookie sheet in the oven and bake at low heat until hard.

Note: The piece may develop cracks and breaks during the baking. If it does, remove it when it is almost hard and fill in the cracks with moist dough while the piece is still very warm. Return it to the oven to finish baking.

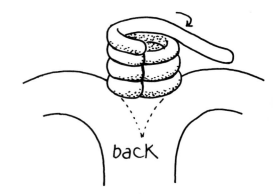

MAKING AND BAKING THE DECORATIONS

Apple (make two): Roll a small aluminum foil ball and cover it smoothly with dough. Form three little leaves and attach them to the top of the apple with dots of water. Insert a paper clip hook in the top.

Bird (make two): Roll a piece of dough to about ½″ thick. Use a cookie cutter to cut out a bird and round off the edges by hand. Incise an eye and some lines in the tail.

Note: All the decorations that follow are cut from dough rolled to ⅛″ thick.

Flower with eight petals: Cut out the flower with a cookie cutter. Incise lines and dots with a wooden skewer.

Scallop-edged flower (make two): Cut flower with scalloped cookie cutter. Incise the lines with the pointed end of a wooden skewer. Make a tiny ball, flatten it and press it onto the center with a dab of water.

Four-part leaf (make two): Cut out an eight-petal flower with a cookie cutter. Cut the flower in half; each half is a four-part leaf. Incise the lines with the point of a wooden skewer.

Leaf (make two): Cut a crescent with a cookie cutter and reshape it slightly to a leaf shape. You can cut a leaf shape by hand (from the rolled dough) or hand-form each leaf. Incise the lines with the point of a wooden skewer.

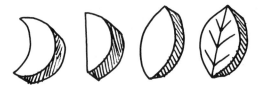

Place all the decorations on a cookie sheet and bake at low heat until hard. Remove when hard and allow to cool.

PAINTING AND FINISHING THE CANDLEHOLDER

Paint the candleholder and all the decorations white, front and back. Let them dry thoroughly and then paint on the bright colors, using the photograph as a guide or inventing your own color scheme. Don't forget the lines on the birds, the dashes on the candle receptacle, the contrasting edging on the scalloped flowers. If you don't have a steady painting hand, eliminate the painted scallops on the base.

When the paint is dry, give the candleholder and all the decorations several coats of polyurethane, allowing each coat to dry thoroughly before applying the next.

When the polyurethane is dry, glue the decorations to the candleholder with epoxy. You'll have to hold each decoration in place while the glue dries. It helps to place the candleholder flat on its back while gluing the flowers in position. Allow the epoxy to dry overnight.

Scalloped Basket

You will need:

1 recipe of flour/salt dough

Ovenproof bowl with flat bottom and a lip around the top edge, about 6″ in diameter, lightly oiled on the outside and on the lip

Rolling pin

Sharp knife

Small flower cookie cutter, about 1½″ across

Wooden skewer or toothpick

Polyurethane, turpentine, brush

Photograph, page 47, for design and color guidance

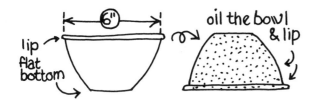

Note: Before beginning, take a close look at the photograph on page 69 for another view of the Scalloped Basket.

MAKING THE COILED PART OF THE BASKET

The coiled part is made with strands rolled to about ¼″ diameter. Roll each strand as you need it. Join new strands to old by cutting the ends on the diagonal, brushing them with water and smoothing them firmly together.

With the bowl upside-down, begin to coil a strand at the center of the flat bottom. Continue to wind the coil, adding more strands if necessary until the bottom of the bowl is covered. End by cutting off the excess strand and then brushing water between the strands to adhere them to each other.

Roll another strand and wrap it around the bowl about 1¼″ below the coil. Join the ends of the strand, cutting off any excess.

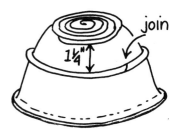

FILLING IN THE SPACE BETWEEN THE COIL AND THE STRAND

Roll another strand and use a sharp knife to cut it into pieces 1″ long. Be sure the ends of each piece are round and neat. Place three pieces next to each other, brush water between the pieces and transfer the unit to the bowl, as shown. Brush water on the three-piece unit to adhere it to the coil and the strand.

Continue in this way, working all around the bowl and making the last three-piece unit fit the remaining gap.

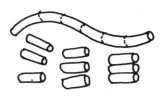

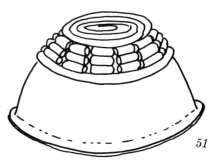

51

MAKING AND ATTACHING THE FLOWERS AND SCALLOPS

Roll dough to ¼″ thick and use the flower-shaped cookie cutter to cut out 15 to 20 flowers. Incise decorative lines on all the flowers, as shown, using two small round caps and the wooden skewer or toothpick.

Attach one flower to the basket by brushing the edge of the flower with water and holding it in place on the bowl until it adheres. Repeat this with a flower placed on each side of the first flower, brushing water between the flowers as well on the top edges of the flowers. Repeat this again so you have five flowers in place.

brush water

Now roll another strand and cut off a section of it long enough to make a scallop from one flower to the next. Press the scallop in place, brushing water on the ends to adhere it to the flowers. Repeat this process of linking the flowers with scallops, making sure to brush water where the scallops touch each other.

brush water

Continue adding flowers and scallops until you have worked all the way around the bowl. The last flower or two will have to be adjusted to fit into the remaining gap.

Press the entire bowl lightly with both hands to ensure that every part is firmly adhered to its neighbors.

BAKING AND FINISHING THE BASKET

Bake at low heat until almost completely hard. Remove from the oven and lift the basket gently from the bowl. Return the basket to the oven to continue baking until completely hard. Remove from the oven and allow to cool.

Brush a coat of sealer (a mixture of one-half turpentine and one-half polyurethane) over the entire basket and allow to dry thoroughly. Then brush on several coats of polyurethane, allowing each coat to dry before applying the next.

Flower Napkin Rings

You will need:

Small amount of flour/salt dough
Wooden napkin rings with flat sides (for examples, see drawing)
Flower-shaped cookie cutter
Garlic press
Rolling pin
Cookie sheet

Acrylic paints, brushes
Small piece of sandpaper
Polyurethane, turpentine
Epoxy glue

Photograph, page 47, for design and color guidance

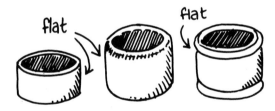

Roll out the dough to ¼″ thick. Use the flower-shaped cookie cutter to cut as many flowers as you have napkin rings. For the center of each flower, force a small amount of dough through the garlic press until the strands are about ⅛″ to ¼″ long. Slide a sharp knife over the garlic press to remove the strands. Brush the center of the flower with water and gently press the strands into place. Transfer the flowers to a cookie sheet.

Bake the flowers at low heat, without turning them over, until they are hard. Remove them from the oven and allow to cool.

Paint the flowers white. When the white is dry, paint them to match your napkins or dishes. While the paint dries, sand a narrow strip on each napkin ring at the point where the flower will be glued. Use epoxy to glue a flower to each ring. Let the epoxy dry completely and then brush several coats of polyurethane on the flower and napkin ring, allowing each coat to dry before applying the next.

Kitchen Memo Board, page 55
Pie Plate Basket, page 58

Kitchen Memo Board

You will need:

1 recipe of bread/glue dough
Food coloring
Sharp knife, wooden skewer or toothpicks
Garlic press

Memo board with wide, flat wood molding
White glue

Photograph, page 54, for design and color guidance

Making the Kitchen Memo Board is simple: Make the bread/glue vegetables; allow them to dry; glue them onto the molding of the memo board. You will have to judge how many vegetables to make for the size and shape of *your* memo board, which may not be exactly like mine. As you make the vegetables, arrange them on the molding in a pleasing design; make as many of each vegetable as your design demands. Let them dry right on the molding. When they are dry, lift each one and apply glue. Replace each vegetable and allow the glue to dry. When all are dry, brush on a coat of polyurethane if you like.

Reminder: Colored dough dries darker than it appears when moist.

Lettuce: Break off a quarter of the dough and color it green. This green will be used for the pea pods and for the tendrils, too.

Roll a ball about ½″ in diameter. Make three small, flat oval leaves by first rolling three small balls and then flattening each one with your fingers. Brush the lower edge of each leaf with water and wrap the leaf around the ball, overlapping the leaves so that the entire ball is wrapped. Continue making and adding slightly larger leaves, brushing them with water and wrapping them around the previous ones. Stagger the placement so the effect is like the leaves of a real lettuce. Curl the top edges out. When the lettuce is large enough—perhaps nine or ten leaves—cut the bottom off with a sharp knife to make a flat underside.

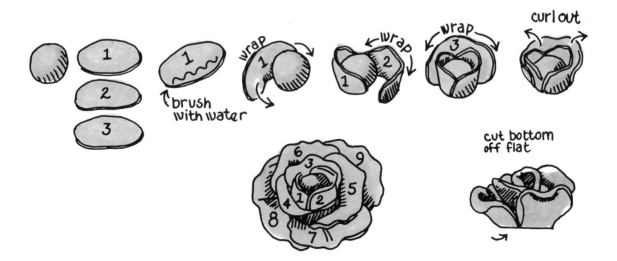

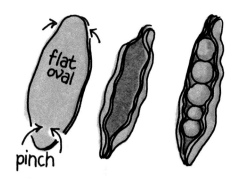

Pea pods: Use the green dough left over from the lettuces. Take a small piece of dough and flatten it to a thin oval about ¾″ x 2″. Fold the ends up and pinch them together to make a little boat-shaped pod. Brush the inside of the pod with water and fill it with little rolled balls.

Tendrils: Use the green dough left over from the lettuces and pea pods. Roll very thin strands, cut them into short lengths and curl them into a variety of spiral shapes (see photograph).

Carrots: Color a small amount of dough orange and another small amount yellow-green. Form two or three orange carrots, each about 1½″ to 2″ long and narrow at the bottom. Press the tops together with dabs of water to make a bunch of carrots. Make the carrot leaves by forcing yellow-green dough through a garlic press. Use a sharp knife or small spatula to remove the leaves in a group, pressing the bottoms together to be sure they will stay in a group. Dab water on the tops of the carrots and gently press the leaves in place.

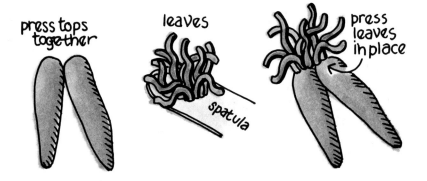

Pumpkin: Use the leftover orange dough with a little more yellow coloring added. Roll a ball and shape it to an oval about 1½″ across. Flatten the back (so it can lie flat on the molding) and then shape the oval so it is more like a pumpkin. Make the vertical lines with the blunt edge of a knife. Add a small green stem, using some leftover green dough and a dab of water.

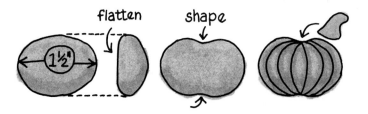

Yellow squash: Color some dough bright yellow. Shape it as shown at right and flatten the back of the squash so it will lie solidly on the molding. Make the markings on the squash: Incise deep lines from top to bottom with the point of a wooden skewer or toothpick; pat the lines together again to make the surface almost smooth. Add a small green stem to the top with a dab of water.

Corn: Break off two pieces of dough. Color one piece yellow and the other piece yellow-green.

Shape a yellow oblong about 2″ to 2¼″ long and about ¾″ square. Round off the square edges and make the top and bottom narrower than the middle. Use a blunt knife edge to make the vertical and horizontal lines.

Make the leaves: Flatten two pieces of green dough, making each about 2¾″ x 1″. Brush the lower part of the corn with water and wrap the leaves around it, one leaf overlapping the other. Curl the edges of the leaves out and down and pinch the leaves together at the bottom of the corn to make a stem.

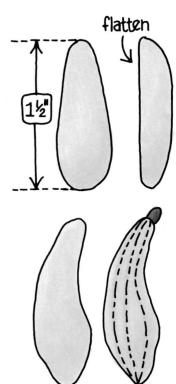

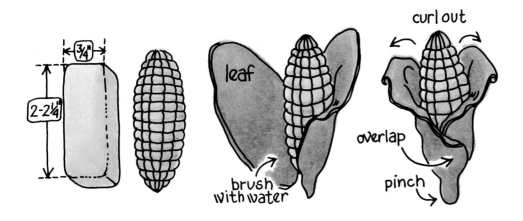

Tomato: Break off a piece of dough and color it dark pinky-red. Make a ball about 1″ in diameter and flatten it on one side so it will lie solidly on the molding. With your finger, make a dent on top and bottom. Use the point of a wooden skewer or toothpick to make the indentations at the top. Dab water on the center indentation and add a tiny green ball for the stem end.

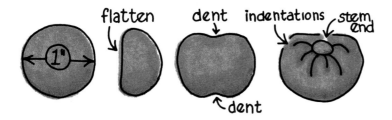

Pie Plate Basket

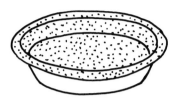

You will need:

1 recipe of flour/salt dough
Pie plate with sloped sides, lightly
    oiled on the inside and on the
    top edge
Rolling pin
Pastry cutter with scalloped blade

Ruler, sharp knife
Small heart-shaped cookie cutter
Polyurethane, turpentine, brush

*Photograph, page 54, for design
and color guidance*

Note: Familiarize yourself with Technique #4, page 15, in Chapter 1. Take a close look at the photograph on page 69 for another view of the Pie Plate Basket.

MAKING THE DOUGH STRIPS AND WEAVING THE BOTTOM OF THE BASKET

Roll the dough out on a floured surface to ⅛" thick in a long rectangle. The rectangle should be at least 3" longer than the measurement of the pie plate from edge to edge.

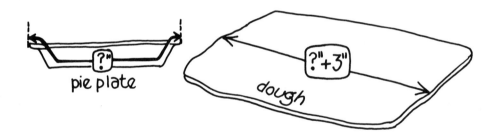

Using the pastry cutter and ruler, cut strips ½" wide. Lay three strips on the pie plate, centered, with ¼" between strips. Lay three more strips on the pie plate, perpendicular and centered, weaving them under and over. Dab water between the strips where they overlap.

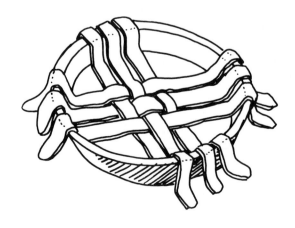

Roll out and cut more dough strips and continue weaving until the bottom of the dish is covered with woven dough. The unwoven ends of the strips should climb neatly up the sides of the pie plate and over the top edge. Adjust the strips so they are evenly spaced all around the sides.

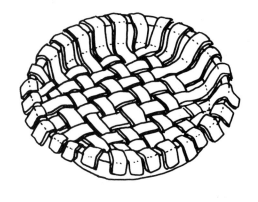

WEAVING AND FINISHING THE SIDES

With a dab of water, join two strips to make one strip long enough to go all the way around the sides of the pie plate. Roll the long strip up and unroll it as you weave it under and over the strips on the sides of the pie plate. Dab water between the strips where they overlap. Join the end of the strip to the beginning of the strip with a dab of water, cutting off any excess.

Use a sharp knife to trim off the excess strips at the top edge of the pie plate.

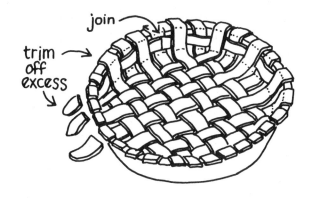

ADDING THE DECORATIONS

Roll out some dough to ⅛″ thick and cut out many small hearts. *Tip:* If you don't have a small heart-shaped cookie cutter, substitute a small flower, bird or other pretty cutter.

Brush water on the end of each dough strip at the top edge of the pie plate. Press hearts into position—touching each other—all around the top edge, as in the photograph on page 54.

BAKING AND FINISHING THE BASKET

Bake at low heat until almost completely hard. Lift the basket gently from the pie plate and return the basket to the oven to continue baking until completely hard. Remove the basket from the oven and allow it to cool.

Brush a coat of sealer (a mixture of one-half turpentine and one-half polyurethane) over the entire basket and allow to dry completely. Then brush on several coats of polyurethane, allowing each coat to dry before applying the next.

Fruit Bowl, page 61

Fruit Bowl

You will need:

1 to 2 recipes of flour/salt dough

Ovenproof bowl with flat bottom and a lip around the top edge, about 6″ to 7″ in diameter, lightly oiled on the outside and on the lip

Rolling pin

Ruler, sharp knife

Acrylic paints, brushes

Polyurethane, turpentine

Photograph, page 60, for design and color guidance

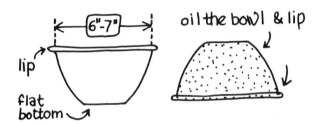

Note: Before you begin, read the general information about flour/salt dough in Chapter 1, giving special attention to Technique #3 on page 15. Take a close look at the photograph on page 69 for another view of the Fruit Bowl.

MAKING THE COILED PART OF THE BOWL

The coiled part is made with strands rolled to about ⅜″ in diameter. Roll each strand as you need it. Join new strands to old by cutting the ends on the diagonal, brushing them with water and smoothing them firmly together.

With the bowl upside-down, begin to coil a strand at the center of the flat bottom. Keep coiling, brushing water between the strands to secure them to each other. Add new strands as needed and continue coiling until you have worked halfway down the bowl. Cut the excess strand off neatly.

Now begin working from the lip up. Place a strand on the lip and begin coiling around the bowl, working up, brushing water on the strand as you go. Continue coiling, adding new strands as needed, until you have three rows. Cut the excess strand off neatly.

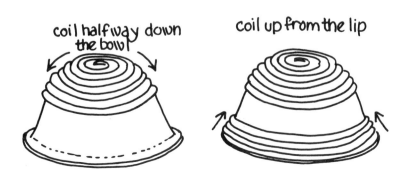

ADDING THE DIAGONAL STRIPS

Roll some dough to ¼″ thick. Cut several strips ½″ wide. Fit pieces of the strips between the coiled sections of the bowl to make the diagonals.

Tip: It will take a certain amount of cutting and recutting to make the diagonals fit properly between the coiled sections. Remember that while it is not important that the diagonal pattern work out perfectly around the bowl, it *is* important that the individual strips fit snugly.

Brush the ends of each strip with water and press the strip firmly in place, wedging it snugly between the coiled sections. Continue working around the bowl, fitting strips in neatly. When you arrive back at the beginning, you will probably find that the pattern does not work out perfectly. Instead of trying to reposition the diagonals, simply add another strip.

Bake at low heat until almost hard. Remove from the oven and lift the dough gently from the bowl. Return the dough to the oven—right side up—to continue baking until completely hard. Take the dough from the oven and allow to cool.

MAKING AND ATTACHING THE HANDLE

This is a little bit tricky. It took me a couple of tries to get the handle right and you may have the same experience.

Measure the diameter inside the bowl and note down the measurement. Roll a strand about ⅝″ in diameter. Shape the strand on the flour-dusted back of a cookie sheet, following the diagram below. Cut off the excess strand and flatten the ends as shown.

shape the strand to make handle

measure inside bowl

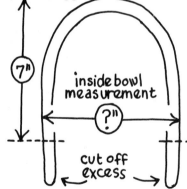

7″

inside bowl measurement

?″

cut off excess

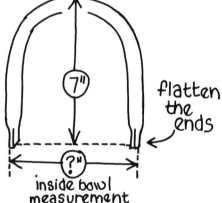

7″

flatten the ends

?″

inside bowl measurement

Check the measurements a second time and adjust if necessary. Bake the handle at low heat for about 20 minutes, just until it is hard enough to turn over. Turn it gently—so that it does not get too flat on one side. Continue baking until completely hard. Remove from the oven and allow to cool.

Hold the cooled handle in the bowl—the flat ends should extend about an inch into the bowl and should just graze the sides. If the flat ends don't fit into the bowl or if they don't reach the sides of the bowl, try the procedure again.

When you have made a correctly sized handle, attach it to the bowl: First, brush water on the flat ends of the handle and on the inside of the bowl where the handle will be attached. Then place a lump of dough over each wet spot inside the bowl and position the handle inside the bowl. The lumps of dough act as mortar between handle and bowl. Make sure the handle is snugly and firmly in place—it should be able to stay up without your holding it. If necessary, build up more dough mortar around the handle. Use a moistened finger to smooth the dough and make the joints neat.

Carefully place the bowl on the lowest rack of the oven and bake at low heat until the mortar is hard. Remove from the oven and allow to cool.

DECORATING THE HANDLE

Roll a strand ¼″ in diameter and long enough to wrap around the handle as you see in the photograph. Brush the handle with water and wrap the strand around it. Finish it off neatly, cutting off any excess strand and smoothing the ends. Bake at low heat until the decoration is hard. Remove from the oven and allow to cool.

FINISHING THE BOWL

Paint the entire basket white. When the white has dried thoroughly, paint the bowl following the design in the photograph, or invent your own color scheme. When the colors are dry, brush on several coats of polyurethane, letting each coat dry completely before applying the next.

Wooden Plate Wall Piece, page 65
Bread Basket, page 67

Wooden Plate Wall Piece

You will need:

1 recipe of flour/salt dough

1 large wooden plate with a wide, flat rim. (The plate used here is 11½″ in diameter with a rim about 1½″ wide.)

Rolling pin

Cookie cutters: miniature boy and girl; small animals (about the size of animal crackers)—duck, cat, dog, rabbit; small heart

Cookie sheet

Sharp knife

Ruler, triangle

Wooden skewer, plastic straw

Polyurethane, turpentine, brushes

Epoxy glue

Photograph, page 64, for design and color guidance

Roll half the dough to ¼″ thick. Cut out as many miniature boys and girls—an equal number of each—as you need to go all around the rim of the plate. Make a few extra, too, so you can pick the best. On each girl, incise eyes and buttons with the blunt end of the wooden skewer and a smile with a split straw. On each boy, incise the same plus a neckline and waistline made with the blunt edge of a knife. Transfer the boys and girls to a flour-dusted cookie sheet.

With the cookie cutters, cut out one of each animal and incise the appropriate eyes, tails, etc. For the tops of the trees, cut out two hearts and compress each one slightly to the shape you see in the photograph. Incise center lines with the blunt edge of a knife. Add a small rectangle to each heart for the trunk, adhering it with water. Transfer the animals and trees to the cookie sheet.

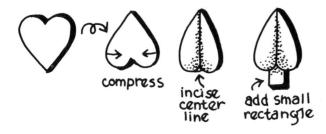

compress   incise center line   add small rectangle

Roll out more dough if necessary. Cut out a house according to the full-sized diagram given below. You may either measure, draw and cut out the house directly on the rolled dough or make a pattern from the diagram (see page 18, Technique #6) and cut around the pattern. It is also possible that this house may be too big for your plate, in which case you must scale it down to fit.

Incise the roof line on the house and then cut the house into two parts as indicated. Cut the door out and replace it in the same opening. Add a small rectangle for the chimney, adhered with a dab of water. Cut out a curved path. Place all the parts of the house on the cookie sheet.

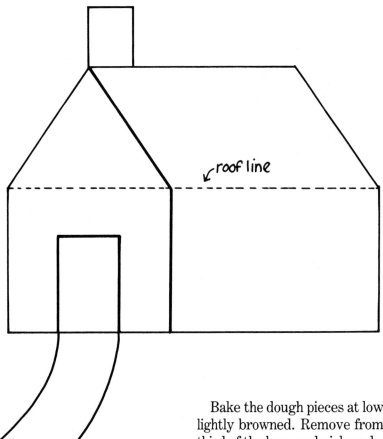

roof line

Bake the dough pieces at low heat, without turning them, until hard and lightly browned. Remove from the oven and allow to cool. Separate out a third of the boys and girls and return them and the two trees to the oven to brown some more at a higher heat. Watch them carefully and remove them when they are medium brown. Allow them to cool.

Brush all the dough pieces with a coat of sealer—a mixture of one-half turpentine and one-half polyurethane. When the sealer is dry, brush on several coats of polyurethane, allowing each coat to dry before applying the next.

When the polyurethane is dry, lay the pieces out on the plate in correct position. Lift each piece, dab it with epoxy glue and replace in position. Let the epoxy dry overnight.

Bread Basket

You will need:

1 recipe of flour/salt dough
Rectangular ovenproof dish with
    sloped sides and a lip around
    the edge, lightly oiled on the
    outside

Rolling pin
Ruler, sharp knife
Polyurethane, turpentine, brush

*Photograph, page 64, for design
and color guidance*

Note: Familiarize yourself with Technique #4 on page 15 of Chapter 1.
Take a close look at the photograph on page 69 for another view of the
Bread Basket.

MAKING THE DOUGH STRIPS AND WEAVING THE BOTTOM OF THE BASKET

Turn the oil-coated dish upside-down and set it aside for now. Roll the
dough out on a floured surface to ⅛″ thick in a long rectangle. Make the
rectangle 3″ longer than the dish measured from end to end.

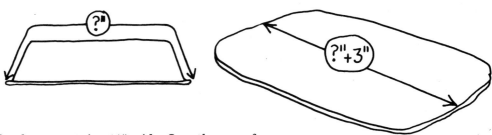

    Using the sharp knife and ruler, cut strips ½″ wide. Lay three or four
strips lengthwise on the dish, centered, with ½″ between strips. Lay three
more strips on the dish, perpendicular and centered, weaving them under
and over. Dab water between the strips where they overlap.

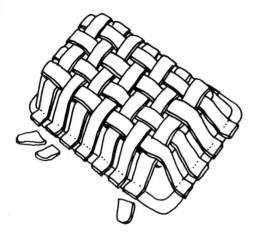

Roll out and cut more dough strips and continue weaving until the bottom of the dish is covered with woven dough. The unwoven ends of the strips should lie neatly on the sides of the dish. Cut off the excess dough at the edge of the lip.

WEAVING AND FINISHING THE SIDES

With a dab of water, join two strips to make one strip long enough to go all the way around the sides of the dish. Roll the long strip up and unroll it as you weave it under and over the strips on the sides of the dish. Brush water between the strips where they overlap. Join the end to the beginning of the strip with a dab of water and cut off any excess strip.

Roll a strand of dough about ½″ in diameter and long enough to reach all the way around the lip of the dish. Starting on one side, place the strand directly on the lip, lifting the end of each strip up and onto the strand. Brush water between the strand and the end of each strip. When you have worked around the whole dish, join the end of the strand to the beginning with a dab of water, cutting off any excess strand, and smooth the joint.

Bake at low heat until almost completely hard. Take the dish from the oven, remove the basket gently from the dish and turn the basket right side up.

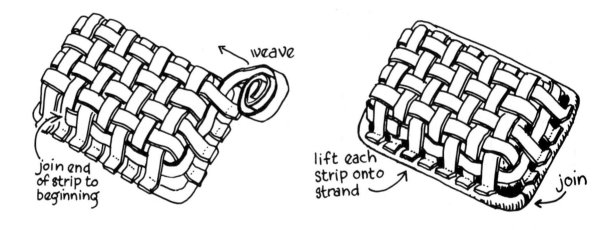

ADDING THE DECORATIONS

While the basket is still very warm, roll many small balls and place them around the top edge, touching each other as in the photograph. Brush water on the edge and between the balls as you place them. Return the basket to the oven and bake until the balls are completely hard. Remove from the oven and allow to cool.

FINISHING THE BASKET

Brush a coat of sealer (a mixture of one-half turpentine and one-half polyurethane) over the entire basket and allow to dry completely. Then brush on several coats of polyurethane, allowing each coat to dry before applying the next.

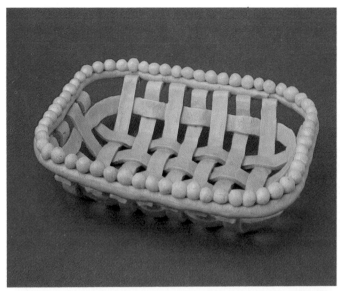

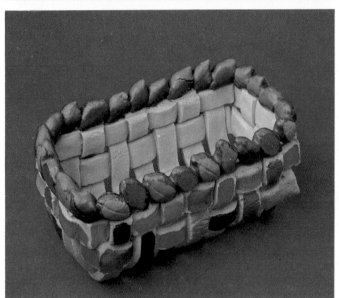

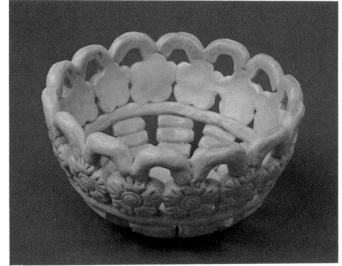

Clockwise from immediate left:
Scalloped Basket, page 51; Planter Basket, page 45;
Bread Basket, page 67; Pie Plate Basket, page 58,
and Fruit Bowl, page 61

Tree-of-Life Wall Piece, page 71

Tree-of-Life Wall Piece

You will need:

1 recipe of flour/salt dough
Cookie sheet
Sharp knife
Rolling pin
Cookie cutters: eight-petal
   flower; five-petal flower;
   scalloped round, about 1½″ in
   diameter; scalloped round,
   about 1″ in diameter; plain
round, about 1″ in diameter;
   small bird; small crescent.
   (You may certainly substitute other
   cutters for the ones above; just be
   sure the general sizes and spirit are
   the same.)

Wooden skewers
Paper clips, wire cutters
Acrylic paints, brushes
Polyurethane, turpentine

*Photograph, page 70, for design
and color guidance*

MAKING THE FOUNDATION

Roll a strand of dough ½″ in diameter and 46″ long. Cut off each end to
shorten the strand to 44″ long. Fold the strand in half and center it on the
flour-dusted back of a cookie sheet. Shape the strand as shown, brushing
water down the center to make a main stem and on the ends of the strand
to adhere them to the main stem.

Roll another strand 9″ long and cut it down to 8″. Roll one more strand
32″ long and cut it into two pieces, each 15″ long. Shape them as shown and
brush them with water at the points of contact.

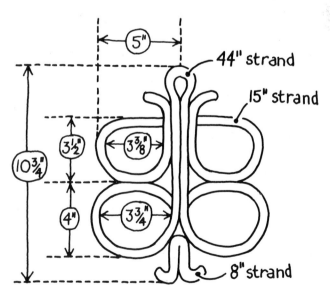

MAKING THE DECORATIONS

Roll dough out to ¼″ to ⅜″ thick. Cut out the following decorations with
cookie cutters and add to them as indicated.

Six birds: Turn three to face left and three to face right. Incise an eye in
each bird.

Four 8-petal flowers: Incise three of them as shown. Cut the fourth in half. Cut the remaining four petals apart.

Six 5-petal flowers: Divide them into three pairs and incise each pair as shown, adding little balls to the center of each flower.

Four plain rounds: Shape two of the rounds at the top to make them more like apples. Poke little holes in the other two rounds to simulate the texture of a lemon. Add a small leaf to the top of each round, as shown, with a dab of water.

Four scalloped rounds, 1½" across: Indent the centers and then incise the lines.

Two scalloped rounds, 1" across: Indent the centers and then incise the lines as shown.

Twelve crescents: Brush the inner edge of each crescent with water and press them together in pairs to make six leaves. Incise with lines as shown.

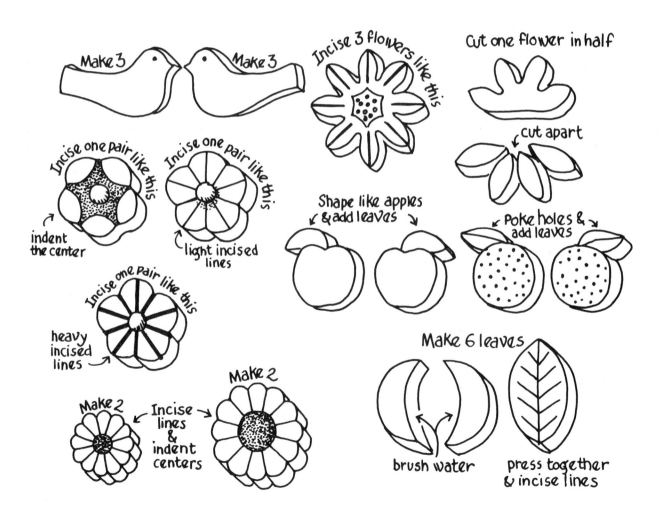

PREPARING THE FOUNDATION AND DECORATIONS FOR BAKING

Apply the decorations to the foundation as shown in the diagram at the right, brushing water between them. With the exception of the decorations perched on the foundation, all the decorations will be resting on the cookie sheet. Add tiny leaves where indicated.

ADDING THE HOOKS AND EYES

Use the wire cutters to cut paper clips (see diagram below left) into twelve U-shaped eyes with long shanks and insert the eyes into the foundation, leaving about ⅛″ to ¼″ extending from the branch. Note that the eye is inserted in the center of the underside. Cut the paper clips into twelve hooks with long shanks and insert them into all four fruits, four flowers (as shown) and four leaves.

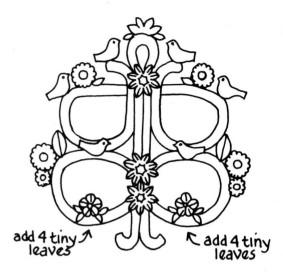

BAKING AND FINISHING THE WALL PIECE

Place all the unattached pieces on the cookie sheet with the foundation, making sure that the hooks don't twist to either side. Bake at low heat (without turning them) until hard. The unattached pieces will be hard before the foundation, so keep an eye on them and remove them when they are done. When the foundation is hard but not done, run a long spatula under it to loosen it from the cookie sheet. Continue baking until completely hard. Remove from the oven and allow the foundation to cool on the cookie sheet.

Paint everything white, front and back. When the white paint is dry, paint on the bright colors, using the photograph for a guide or inventing your own color scheme. When the paint is thoroughly dry, brush on several coats of polyurethane, allowing each coat to dry before applying the next.

Hang the dangling decorations from their hooks and hang the wall piece by its loop.

Sugar Paste Vase, page 75

Sugar Paste Vase

You will need:

2 recipes of sugar paste dough
  (keep the batches separate)

Food coloring

Glass jar with straight sides, with
  label and residual glue
  removed. I used a large peanut
  butter jar.

Sharp knife

Rolling pin

Cookie cutters: small heart;
  scalloped round, about 2½″ in
  diameter

Tweezers, toothpicks

Colored non-pareils (tiny candy
  dots)

White glue

Tissue paper

*Photograph, page 74, for design
  and color guidance*

Reminder: When you use this vase, be careful not to splash water on the sugar paste. Always fill the vase halfway, using a small pitcher. Never fill the vase under the faucet!

MAKING THE BASIC COILED VASE

Separate out a quarter of one batch of dough; color that quarter green and the rest yellow. *Reminder:* The dough dries lighter than it appears when moist.

Follow the directions for coiling explained in Technique #4 on page 31 of Chapter 1. Work around the jar with yellow strands until you have covered two-thirds of the jar. Then switch to green strands for three or four rounds (about an inch) and back to yellow for the final few rounds. End the coiling where the jar indents for the threaded section (where the lid screws on).

Roll green balls, flatten them slightly and press them into place around the top edge. Be sure to brush the topmost yellow strand with water before applying the green balls and brush water on each ball where it joins its neighbor. Set the vase aside to dry overnight.

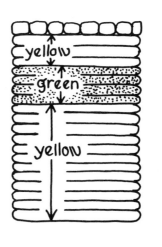

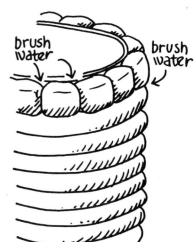

MAKING THE PARTS OF THE DECORATIONS

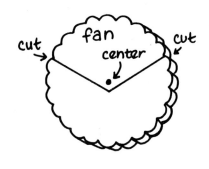

You'll need the green and yellow dough left over from the vase and some uncolored dough, too. Break off three pieces of the uncolored dough and color them lavender, pink and blue. Make the parts of the decorations and place them on waxed paper to dry overnight, turning occasionally so they dry evenly.

Blue: Make 20 to 25 petals, each about ½″ long—each petal is a small oval rolled between your fingers and flattened, pointier at one end. Make 5 to 10 small ovals, like rice kernels. Make and flatten several small balls. Roll dough to ⅛″ thick and use the scalloped cookie cutter to cut one round; cut the round down to a fan shape as shown.

Pink: Roll 20 to 25 balls and flatten each ball; these are the disks that decorate the green band, so be sure they will fit on it as in the photograph. Make 15 to 20 small ovals, like rice kernels. Roll several small balls for the centers of the flowers; flatten two or three of them. Roll dough to ⅛″ thick and use heart cookie cutter to cut several small hearts.

Lavender: Roll 15 to 20 small balls and flatten each.

Yellow: Roll 20 to 25 small balls and flatten each slightly.

Green: Make five or six leaves—roll ovals and flatten between your fingers.

White: Roll ten tiny balls.

JOINING THE PARTS TO MAKE THE DECORATIONS

When all the parts are dry, glue together as specified in 1, 2 and 3 below. Use a toothpick for applying the white glue and tweezers for lifting each part and putting it in position on the glue. Allow the glue to dry thoroughly.

1. Glue one flattened yellow ball to each pink disk.

2. With a toothpick, draw a line of glue on the front and along the top of each of two pink hearts. Dip each heart in colored non-pareils. Glue a flattened blue ball to the point of each heart.

3. Decorate the fan as shown in the photograph on page 74.

GLUING ALL THE DECORATIONS TO THE VASE

Rest the vase on its side on a soft bed of tissue paper. Glue the pink/yellow disks to the green band as in the photograph. You will only be able to apply about four at a time because they must dry before you can turn the vase. Proceed slowly with this until you have worked around the entire vase.

When all the glue is dry, rest the jar with its best side up and begin to glue on the other decorations as in the photo. Start with the hearts, the fan and the blue flower that goes above the green band. Allow the glue to dry.

Rotate the vase slightly and glue on the decorations that go to the right of the fan. Allow the glue to dry. Rotate the vase in the opposite direction and glue on the flowers and other decorations that go to the left of the fan. Allow the glue to dry completely.

Christmas Decorations

As you can see from the photographs, doughcraft decorations promote the Christmas spirit all around the house. Many of the projects in this chapter are ornaments; instructions are given for making one of each design, but you will probably want to make multiples of the ones you like. If you are making a variety of flour/salt dough ornaments, remember that you can bake many ornaments at the same time, on the same cookie sheet. See page 121 for instructions on how to hang the ornament you make.

Important: Before beginning any project, check which kind of dough you'll be using and familiarize yourself with the general information about it in Chapter 1.

Folk Art Ornaments:
Star and Heart, page 80;
Christmas Tree, page 81

Christmas tree at left is decorated
with ornaments featured in this
section—see pages 80 through 89.
Dough ornaments are also used to
trim the gaily wrapped packages;
to see how this is done, turn to
page 90.

Folk Art Star Ornament

You will need:

Small amount of flour/salt dough
Rolling pin
Star cookie cutter
Aspic cutters: flower; leaf
Plastic straw, wooden skewer
Cookie sheet

Acrylic paints, brushes
Polyurethane, turpentine
Ribbon, cord or yarn

*Photograph, page 79, for design
and color guidance*

Roll the dough out to ⅛" thick and cut a star with the cookie cutter. Use the plastic straw to make a hole in one point of the star.

Roll some dough thinner than ⅛" and use the aspic cutters to cut three flowers and six leaves. Incise a center hole in each flower and a center line on each leaf. Brush the star with water and arrange the flowers and leaves, checking the photograph for positioning. Roll tiny balls and add them with dots of water.

Place the star on a flour-dusted cookie sheet and bake at low heat until hard. Remove from the oven and allow to cool. Paint the star white, let the white paint dry and then paint it with colors. Follow the photograph or invent your own color scheme, and don't forget the contrasting edge. When the paint is dry, brush on several coats of polyurethane, letting each coat dry thoroughly before applying the next.

Hang with ribbon, cord or yarn.

Folk Art Heart Ornament

You will need:

Small amount of flour/salt dough
Rolling pin
Cookie cutters: large heart;
    medium heart (optional). (If you
    don't have the large heart
    cutter, use the pattern on the
    opposite page.)
Aspic cutters: crescent; flower

Sharp knife
Cookie sheet
Wooden skewer, plastic straw
Acrylic paints, brushes
Polyurethane, turpentine
Narrow grosgrain ribbon

*Photograph, page 79, for design
and color guidance*

Roll the dough out to ⅛" thick. Cut out a large heart, using either a cookie cutter or the pattern opposite (see page 18 for instructions on transferring patterns). Cut the center from the large heart, using either a medium heart cutter or a sharp knife; the remaining heart should be about ¾" wide from outer to inner edge. Use plastic straw to make a hole at the top of the heart. Transfer the heart to the back of a flour-dusted cookie sheet.

Make the decorations for the heart. Each tulip-shaped flower is made by cutting a leaf with the aspic cutter and bending it as shown; make 18 to 20 tulips. Cut five or six flowers with the aspic cutter and make a center hole in each with the blunt end of a wooden skewer. The leaves are shaped by hand and incised with the blunt edge of a knife; make 8 to 10 leaves. Roll thin strands for the stems.

Brush the heart with water and arrange the flowers, leaves and stems on it, following the photograph for positioning. Bake the heart at low heat until hard. Remove it from the oven and allow it to cool.

Paint the heart white. When the white paint is dry, paint on the colors you see in the photograph or invent your own color scheme. Paint the background first, then the leaves and finally the flowers. When the paint is thoroughly dry, brush on several coats of polyurethane, allowing each coat to dry before applying the next.

Hang the ornament with ribbon.

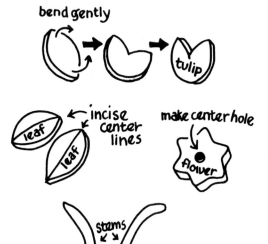

Folk Art Christmas Tree Ornament

You will need:

Small amount of flour/salt dough

Tracing paper, carbon paper and thin cardboard for making pattern

Rolling pin

Sharp knife

Aspic cutters; crescent; flower

Wooden skewer

Cookie sheet

Acrylic paints, brushes

Polyurethane, turpentine

Satin ribbon or gold cord

Photograph, page 79, for design and color guidance

Transfer the pattern to thin cardboard and cut it out. (See page 18 for instructions on making and using patterns.) Roll the dough out to ⅛" thick and use the pattern to cut out the basic tree. Transfer the tree to the back of a flour-dusted cookie sheet. Cut ten little triangles and custom-fit them on the sides of the tree, turning up the points jauntily. Brush water between the triangles and the tree to adhere them.

Make the decorations for the basic tree, following the diagram below for details and positioning: Roll the dough to thinner than ⅛″ and use the aspic cutter to cut out four flowers. Make a hole in one flower and adhere it to the top of the tree. Incise the other three flowers as shown. Cut four crescents and incise them as shown. Hand-model 8 to 10 tiny leaves and incise center lines with the point of a wooden skewer. Roll tiny balls for the lower edge and poke them in place with the point of the skewer. Brush the tree with water and arrange all the elements as shown in the diagram.

Bake the tree at low heat until hard. Remove from the oven and allow to cool. Paint the entire tree white and then, when the white paint is dry, paint it in bright colors. When all paint is completely dry, brush on several coats of polyurethane, allowing each coat to dry before brushing on the next.

Hang the ornament with satin ribbon or gold cord.

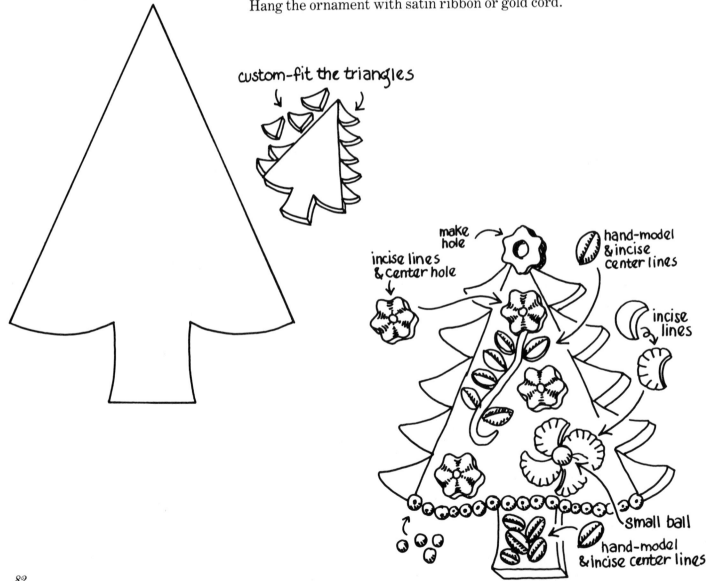

custom-fit the triangles

make hole

incise lines & center hole

hand-model & incise center lines

incise lines

small ball

hand-model & incise center lines

Little Christmas Tree Ornament

Snowman Ornament

Star/Bell/Candy Cane Garland #1

Star / Bell / Candy Cane Garland #1

You will need:

1 recipe (or more) of flour/salt
   dough

Rolling pin

Cookie cutters: small star; small
   bell

Cookie sheet

Sharp knife

Wooden skewer

Acrylic paints, brushes

Polyurethane, turpentine

Thin cord

*Drawing, above, for design and
   color guidance*

Note: If you want to make enough garland to cover your whole Christmas
tree, make several recipes of flour/salt dough.

MAKING THE STARS AND BELLS

Divide the dough in half, rewrap one half and set it aside for the candy
canes. Use the remaining half for the stars and bells.

Roll out small amounts of dough to ⅛" thick and cut out three stars or bells at a time. Make a stringing hole in each piece—make the hole immediately, before the dough forms a dry crust. Use the blunt end of a wooden skewer to make each hole, rotating the skewer in the hole to enlarge it. Turn each piece over, insert the skewer from the back and rotate it to make a clean hole. Make the hole larger in diameter than the cord since the hole will close up slightly during baking. Repeat the process to make an equal number of stars and bells.

Transfer the stars and bells to a flour-dusted cookie sheet.

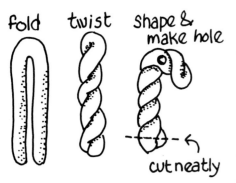

fold   twist   shape & make hole

cut neatly

MAKING THE CANDY CANES

Make the candy canes with the remaining dough. For each cane, roll a strand 9" long and ¼" in diameter. Fold it in half and twist the strand as shown. Place the twisted strand on the cookie sheet and shape it into a candy cane. Cut the lower ends off neatly. Make three canes at a time and make a hole in each as described above.

BAKING, FINISHING AND STRINGING THE STARS, BELLS AND CANDY CANES

Bake the dough pieces at low heat until hard, turning once during baking. Remove from the oven and allow to cool. Paint all the pieces white, let them dry and then paint them with bright colors as shown in the drawing on the preceding page. When the paint is dry, brush on several coats of polyurethane, allowing each coat to dry completely before applying the next.

Note: Be sure the stringing holes do not clog up with paint or polyurethane.

Cut 6- or 8-foot lengths of ribbon or cord and string the stars, bells and candy canes: String on a star and tie a double knot to secure it. Skip three inches of ribbon or cord, string a bell and tie a double knot. Skip three more inches, string a candy cane and tie a double knot. Repeat this sequence to the end of the ribbon or cord.

Little Christmas Tree Ornament

You will need:

Small amount of flour/salt dough
Rolling pin
Christmas tree cookie cutter
Cookie sheet
Acrylic paints, brushes

Polyurethane, turpentine
Ribbon, cord or yarn
Drawing, page 83, for design and color guidance

Roll the dough out to ⅛" thick and cut a tree with the cookie cutter. Make the leaves for the tree: Roll small balls, flatten them and apply them to the tree with water; work from the bottom of the tree up to the top, overlapping the leaves. For the decorations, roll small balls and attach them to the tree with dabs of water. Place the tree on a flour-dusted cookie sheet.

Bake the tree at low heat until hard. Remove from the oven and allow to cool. Paint the entire tree white, allow the white to dry and paint it with bright colors. When all paint is dry, brush on several coats of polyurethane, letting each coat dry before brushing on the next.

Hang the ornament with ribbon, cord or yarn.

Snowman Ornament

You will need:

Small amount of flour/salt dough
Plastic straw
Garlic press
Cookie sheet
Acrylic paints, brushes

Polyurethane, turpentine
Ribbon, cord or yarn

Drawing, page 83, for design and color guidance

Roll two balls of dough and flatten them slightly; the larger (the body) should measure about 2¼″ in diameter and the smaller (the head) should measure about 1½″ in diameter. Join the head and body with water. Brush water on the sides of the body and add two small balls for arms. Roll a small strand of dough and cut a small rectangle of dough; brush them with water and add them to the top of the head to make a hat. Use the plastic straw to make a hole in the hat. For the scarf, roll strands ¼″ in diameter, brush the neckline and body with water and apply the strands as shown. Force a bit of dough through the garlic press, lift some squiggly strands from the press and adhere them to the tips of the scarf. Roll small balls for the eyes, nose and buttons and a tiny strand for the mouth and adhere them to the snowman with water.

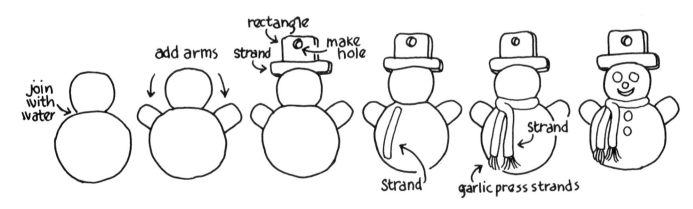

Transfer the snowman to the flour-dusted cookie sheet. Bake the snowman at low heat until hard, remove from the oven and allow to cool. Paint the entire snowman white and let the paint dry. Then paint the snowman as you see it in the color drawing or invent a color scheme of your own. When the paint is dry, brush on several coats of polyurethane, letting each coat dry before applying the next.

Hang the ornament with ribbon, cord or yarn.

Berry Wreath Ornament

OpenWork Bird Ornament

Gold Ring/Gold Star Ornament

Braided Wreath Ornament

Openwork Bird Ornament

You will need:

Small amount of flour/salt dough

Tracing paper, carbon paper and thin cardboard for making pattern

Cookie sheet

Crayon or grease pencil

Acrylic paints (one color plus silver), brushes

Polyurethane, turpentine

Ribbon

Drawing, page 86, for design and color guidance

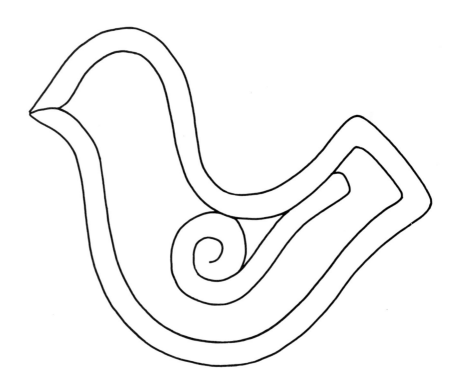

Transfer the pattern to thin cardboard and cut it out (see page 18 for instructions on making and using patterns). Place the cardboard pattern on a cookie sheet and outline it with crayon or grease pencil. Roll dough into a strand 14″ long and ¼″ in diameter. Shape the strand over the outline on the cookie sheet and join the ends of the strand with water at the beak, cutting off any excess strand. Roll another strand about 5″ long and ¼″ in diameter. Shape it like the bird's wing on the pattern and cut off any excess. Move the wing over to the cookie sheet and attach it to the bird with water. Roll four balls for the tail, four for the crest and one for the eye; adhere them to the bird with water.

Bake the bird at low heat until hard, turning it once during baking. Remove it from the oven and allow it to cool. Paint the bird white and let it dry. Then paint the bird one color and the crest, eye, wing and tail decorations silver. When all paint is thoroughly dry, brush on several coats of polyurethane, allowing each coat to dry before applying the next.

Hang the ornament with ribbon.

Braided Wreath Ornament

You will need:

Small amount of flour/salt dough
Cookie sheet
Polyurethane, turpentine, brush
Ribbon, 1″ wide and about 12″
   long

White glue
Ribbon, cord or yarn

*Drawing, page 86, for design and
color guidance*

Divide the dough into three equal parts. Roll each part into a strand ½″ in diameter and about 16″ long. Transfer the strands to a flour-dusted cookie sheet and braid them without stretching the dough. Shape the braid into a circle 4″ in diameter, cut off the ends neatly and join the ends with water.

Bake the wreath at low heat until it is hard. Remove from the oven and allow to cool. Brush the wreath with a coat of sealer (a mixture of one-half polyurethane and one-half turpentine) and let the sealer dry. Brush the wreath with several coats of polyurethane, allowing each coat to dry before applying the next. When the polyurethane is thoroughly dry, tie the ribbon in a bow and glue it over the spot where the strands were joined. Trim the ends of the ribbon.

Hang the ornament with ribbon, cord or yarn.

Berry Wreath Ornament

You will need:

Small amount of flour/salt dough
Toothpick
Cookie sheet
Acrylic paints, brushes
Polyurethane, turpentine

Ribbon, ⅜″ wide and about 7″
   long
White glue
Ribbon, cord or yarn

*Drawing, page 86, for design and
color guidance*

Roll 15 to 20 balls of dough ranging in size from ½″ in diameter to ⅞″ in diameter. Working on a flour-dusted cookie sheet, brush the balls with water and put them together in a wreath shape about 3¼″ in diameter. Press the berries gently as you attach them, to make a flattened underside. Use the toothpick to make a small indentation on each berry.

Model ten leaves by hand; each one should be about ⅛″ thick and ¾″ long. Brush the end of each leaf with water and tuck it under the berries, pressing them together to adhere them.

Bake the wreath at low heat until it is hard. Remove it from the oven and allow it to cool. Paint the wreath white and when the white paint is thoroughly dry, paint it with bright colors as in the drawing. Allow the paint to dry and then brush on several coats of polyurethane, letting each coat dry before applying the next. Tie the 7″ ribbon in a small bow and glue the bow to the wreath. Hang the ornament with ribbon, cord or yarn.

Gold Ring/Gold Star Ornament

You will need:

Small amount of flour/salt dough
Rolling pin
Cookie cutters: round, about 2¾"
    in diameter; round, about 2¼"
    in diameter; small star, about
    1¾" wide; aspic cutter star
Wooden skewer
Cookie sheet

Acrylic paints (white, gold),
    brushes
Polyurethane, turpentine
Thin gold cord, gold thread

*Drawing, page 86, for design and
    color guidance*

Roll the dough out to ⅛" thick. Use the larger round to cut a circle and transfer it to a flour-dusted cookie sheet. Use the smaller round to cut out the center of the circle, leaving a ring about ¼" wide. Cut a small star from the leftover round of dough and transfer it to the cookie sheet, too. Use the aspic cutter to cut a tiny star from the center of the small star. With the blunt end of the skewer, make a hanging hole in the ring (the hole should be larger in diameter than the cord) and in the star.

cut out center   make hole   cut out star   cut out tiny star   make hole

ring ¼" wide

Bake the ring and star at low heat until hard; turn them once during baking. Remove from the oven and allow to cool. Paint both pieces white and when the white paint is dry, brush on two coats of gold paint. When the gold is dry, brush on several coats of polyurethane. Let each coat dry before applying the next. Be sure that the holes do not clog up with paint or polyurethane.

Suspend the star from the ring with a small loop of gold thread. Tie a loop of gold cord through the hole in the ring.

loop of gold thread   loop of gold cord

Package Trims

The brightly wrapped packages shown below are trimmed with the usual ribbon plus an extra treat—a pretty dough ornament which can be saved and hung on the Christmas tree. Attach the ornament to the package by first tying or gluing a loop of thin string or cord to the ornament and then threading the ribbon through the loop before tying the ribbon in a bow.

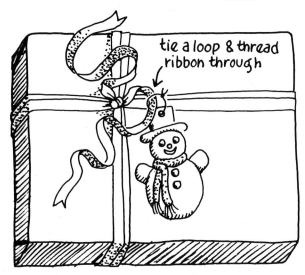

tie a loop & thread
ribbon through

When you remove the ornament from the package, replace the thin string with a larger loop of ribbon, cord or yarn and hang it on the tree.

Christmas gifts
with doughcraft
package trims

Christmas Cookies, page 92

Christmas Cookies

You will need:

1 recipe (or more) of cookie
   dough

1 recipe of decorating icing

Food coloring

Pastry bags

Icing tips, one round and one
   star

Christmas cookie cutters: five-
   and six- pointed stars; candy
   canes; Christmas tree

Other cookie cutters: diamond;
   doughnut, 2¾″ in diameter, for
   wreath; miniature boy and
   miniature girl; bell, medium-
   sized heart and 1″-diameter
   round for making the angels

*Photograph, page 91, for
additional design and color
guidance.*

Roll out the dough and cut out as many or as few of each shape as you like.

Tip: To make an angel, cut out one bell, one heart and one small round.
Combine them as shown in the drawing, using a little water as glue and
pressing the parts firmly together.

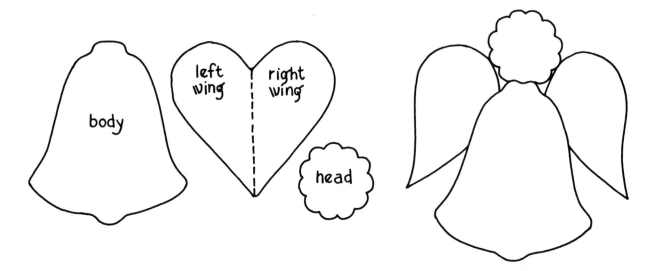

Bake the cookies according to the recipe and allow them to cool while you
prepare one batch of decorating icing. Divide the icing into small bowls and
tint each a different color—pink, blue, lavender, yellow, green—leaving
one bowl white. Cover the bowls tightly with plastic wrap. Prepare the
pastry bags by filling each one half full of icing as described in Chapter 1.
Attach round tip to one bag and star tip to another. Decorate cookies.

Use the photographs for design and color inspiration but don't be afraid
to try some ideas of your own. The diagrams opposite show you some of
my designs and which tip to use for each part.

Note: The Christmas tree cookies are decorated in the same way as the
gingerbread trees around the Gingerbread House (see page 104) but
with icing stars and dots instead of candies.

Tip: Do as much decorating as you can with one icing tip coupled to one color before you switch to the next. For example, attach the round tip to the bag of lavender icing. Pipe the decorations on all the angels' wings, then use the same tip and icing to do part of the stars, a repeat stripe on the candy canes and perhaps a couple of outlines on the diamonds. Continue in this way with each color, alternating the tips. There will be some backtracking as you complete your designs but you'll keep it to a minimum if you use this technique. Allow the icing to dry before serving the cookies.

Pink = round tip
Blue = star tip
Light brown = cookie

Noel Tree, page 95

Noel Tree

You will need:

1 recipe of flour/salt dough
Rolling pin
Cookie cutters: scalloped round,
    2½" in diameter; small star,
    about 1¾" wide; small heart,
    about 1¼" wide
Plastic straw

Cookie sheet
Acrylic paints, brushes
Polyurethane, turpentine
Glitter (red, gold and silver)

*Photograph, page 94, for design
    and color guidance*

MAKING THE BASIC TREE

Roll the dough out to ¼" thick. With the scalloped cookie cutter, cut sixteen
rounds. Lay them out on the flour-dusted back of a cookie sheet as shown.
Brush water between the rounds and press them firmly together to be sure
they all stick to each other.

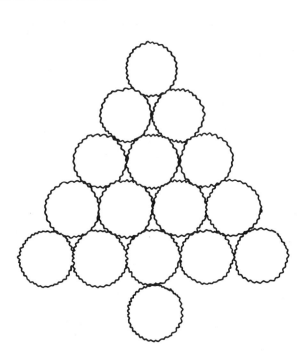
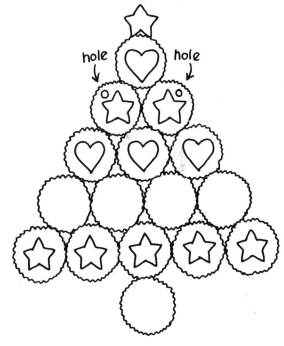

Roll the remaining dough out to ⅛" thick. Cut out seven stars and four
hearts. Brush water on the back of each and center each on a round as in
the photograph. Cut an eighth star and adhere it with water to the top of
the tree.

Use the plastic straw to make holes for hanging the tree, as shown above
right.

MAKING THE LETTERS

Each letter is made from strands of dough rolled to about ⅜″ in diameter. Form the strands into letters 1½″ high, as in the diagram.

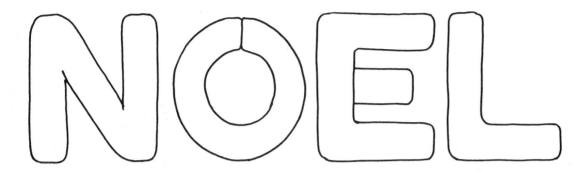

Brush each round with water and set each letter in position on the moistened round.

BAKING AND REINFORCING THE TREE

Bake the tree at low heat until hard. Do not turn it over during baking, but halfway through baking run a long spatula under the tree to loosen it from the cookie sheet. When the tree is hard, remove it from the oven, let it cool until you can handle it and very carefully turn it over on the cookie sheet. On the back of the still-warm tree, press a small ball of dough over every spot where the rounds touch. These flattened balls reinforce the joints.

Return the tree to the oven, upside-down, and bake at low heat until the new dough is hard. Remove from the oven and allow to cool.

PAINTING AND FINISHING THE TREE

Paint the entire piece white, front and back. When the white is dry, paint the tree green, the bottom round brown, the hearts red, the stars yellow and the letters white (a second coat). Let the colors dry.

Apply the glitter: Brush the heart with polyurethane and sprinkle with red glitter while the polyurethane is still wet. Allow the polyurethane to dry and then blow or tap the excess glitter off. Repeat with red glitter on the tree trunk, gold glitter on the stars and silver glitter on the letters.

When the polyurethane is completely dry, brush several more coats of polyurethane on the entire tree, allowing each coat to dry before applying the next.

Ornaments based on musical instruments:
Violin, page 98;
Drum, page 99;
French Horn, page 100

Violin Ornament

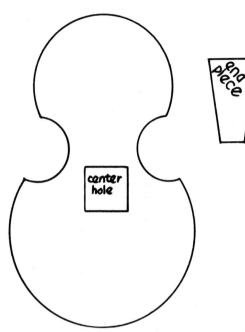

You will need:

Small amount of flour/salt dough

Tracing paper, carbon paper and thin cardboard for making pattern

Rolling pin

Sharp knife

Cookie sheet

Acrylic paints (red, green, and gold), brushes

Polyurethane, turpentine

Red embroidery thread

White glue

Flat gold cord

Photograph, page 97, for design and color guidance

Transfer the pattern to thin cardboard and cut it out (see page 18 for instructions on making and using patterns). Roll the dough out to 1/8" thick and use the pattern and a sharp knife to cut out the violin body and the end piece. Cut out the center hole with a sharp knife (or an aspic cutter) as shown in the pattern. For the neck of the violin, roll a strand 2 1/4" long and 3/8" in diameter. Flatten one half of the strand slightly and trim the sides as shown. Roll four tiny balls. Use water to attach the neck, the end piece and the tiny balls.

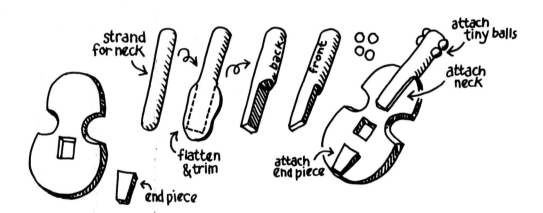

Transfer the violin to the cookie sheet; bake at low heat until hard. Remove from the oven and allow to cool. Paint the violin white and when the white is dry, paint the violin red, green and gold as shown (it will need two coats of each). When all paint is dry, brush on several coats of polyurethane, allowing each coat to dry before applying the next. For the violin strings, cut three pieces of embroidery thread and glue them to the neck and the end piece.

Hang the ornament with a loop of flat gold cord.

Drum Ornament

You will need:

Small amount of flour/salt dough
Rolling pin
Round cookie cutter, 2¾″ in
    diameter
Toothpick
Cookie sheet

Acrylic paints (red, green, gold
    and silver), brushes
Polyurethane, turpentine
Flat gold cord

*Photograph, page 97, for design
    and color guidance*

Roll the dough out to ⅛″ thick. Use the cookie cutter to cut out a circle and then cut off the sides of the circle. Roll a strand about ¼″ in diameter and flatten it with the rolling pin. Brush water on the drum as shown and press pieces of the flattened strand on the drum. Turn the drum wrong side up and trim off the excess strand, allowing it to extend slightly beyond the sides of the drum. Turn the drum back to the right side and smooth the edges of the strand.

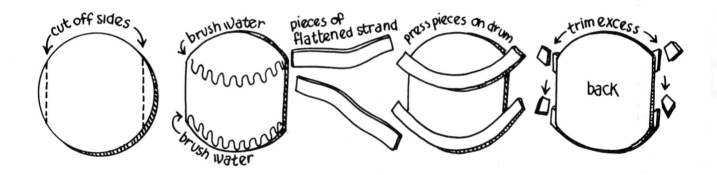

Roll a little piece of dough to a very skinny strand. Cut off seven tiny pieces and apply them to the flat bands by spearing each piece with a toothpick and placing it in position with a dab of water. Roll another piece of dough to a long skinny strand. Brush the middle section of the drum with water and shape the skinny strand, as shown in the photograph on page 97. Cut off any excess strand.

Transfer the drum to a flour-dusted cookie sheet and bake it at low heat until hard. Remove from the oven and allow it to cool. Paint the drum white and when the white is dry, paint it red, green, gold and silver as shown (it will need two coats of each). When all paint is dry, brush on several coats of polyurethane, allowing each coat to dry before applying the next.

Hang the ornament with a loop of flat gold cord.

French Horn Ornament

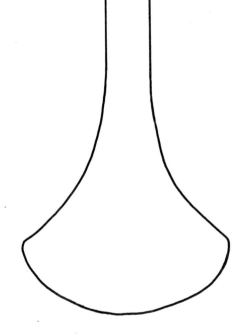

You will need:

Small amount of flour/salt dough

Tracing paper, carbon paper and thin cardboard for making pattern

Rolling pin

Sharp knife

Cookie sheet

Acrylic paints (red and gold), brushes

Polyurethane, turpentine

Flat gold cord

Photograph, page 97, for design and color guidance

Transfer the pattern to thin cardboard and cut it out (see page 18 for instructions on making and using patterns). Roll the dough out to ⅛″ thick and use the pattern and a sharp knife to cut out the horn. Curve the horn as shown in the photograph on page 97, brushing it with water at the overlap. Roll a short strand about ⅜″ in diameter; brush the end of the horn with water, press the strand on the edge and cut off any excess. Add a small oval ball of dough for the mouthpiece. Transfer the horn to a flour-dusted cookie sheet.

Bake the horn at low heat until hard. Remove from the oven and allow to cool. Paint the horn white and when the white is dry, paint the horn red and gold as shown (it will need two coats of each). When the paint is dry, brush on several coats of polyurethane, letting each coat dry before applying the next.

Hang the ornament with a loop of flat gold cord.

Lamb and Lion Ornaments

Lamb and Lion Ornaments

You will need:

½ recipe of flour/salt dough
Wooden skewer
Garlic press
Sharp knife
Plastic straw

Cookie sheet
Polyurethane, turpentine, brush
Ribbon

*Photograph, above, for design and
   color guidance*

MAKING THE LAMB

Make and put together the parts of the lamb's body first, then add the fleece.

Body: Roll an oval and press it flat on one side. (The flat side will be the back.) It should then measure about 2″ long and 1¼″ high.

Head: Roll a smaller oval (about the size of a grape), flatten it on one side and attach it to the body with a bit of water. Smooth the joint. Roll a little ball for the ear, flatten it and attach it to the head with water. Note that the ear points down. Incise an eye and a nostril with the blunt end of the wooden skewer.

Legs: Roll four small cylinders and pinch the end of each to a point. Attach the legs to the body with dabs of water.

Tail: Roll a small cylinder and attach it to the body.

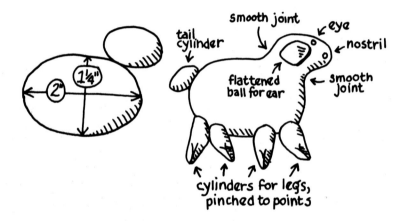

Fleece: Force small amounts of dough through the garlic press to make strands about ¼″ to ⅜″ long. Run a sharp knife over the press to remove each group of strands. Brush the lamb's body with water and gently press the strands in place all over the body as shown in the photograph.

Use the plastic straw to make a hole for hanging the lamb. Transfer the lamb to a flour-dusted cookie sheet.

MAKING THE LION

Make and put together the parts of the lion's body first, then add the mane.

Body: Roll an oval and press it flat on the side. It should then measure about 3″ long and 1¾″ high. Use the plastic straw to make a hole in the lion's back.

Head: Roll a sphere about the size of a grape and press it flat on one side. Adhere it to the body with water, as shown in the drawing.

Legs: Roll four cylinders (two short and two slightly longer) and adhere them to the body with water. Use the blunt end of the skewer to incise the toenails.

Tail: Roll a narrow cylinder, adhere it to the body with water and curve it as shown.

Face: Roll two little balls of dough for the cheeks, flatten them and adhere them to the head with water. Poke dots in the cheeks with the point of the skewer. Roll tiny balls for the eyes and nose, flatten them and adhere them with water as shown.

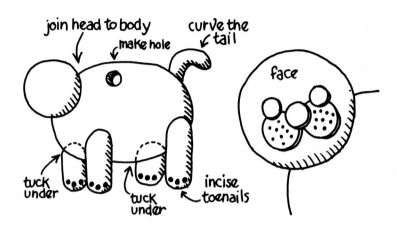

Mane: Force small amounts of dough through the garlic press to make strands about ½″ to ¾″ long. Run a sharp knife over the press to remove each group of strands. Brush water around the lion's face and gently press strands in place, as shown in the photograph.

Tail: Brush the tip of the lion's tail with water and place on it a few strands from the garlic press.

Transfer the lion to the cookie sheet.

BAKING AND FINISHING THE ANIMALS

Bake the animals at low heat until hard and lightly browned. Remove them from the oven and allow them to cool. Brush them with sealer (a mixture of one-half polyurethane and one-half turpentine) and let the sealer dry. Brush on several coats of polyurethane, letting each coat dry before applying the next.

Hang the ornaments with ribbon.

*Christmas tree above is decorated with ornaments featured
on pages 105 through 109.
The Gingerbread House beneath the tree appears on pages 110 to 113.*

Ruffled Fan Ornament

You will need:

Small amount of sugar paste dough

Food coloring

Rolling pin

Scalloped round cookie cutter, 4″ in diameter

Aspic cutter flower

Wooden skewer

Lace ruffle, ½″ wide and 5″ long

White glue, tweezers

Narrow satin ribbon

Adjoining photograph for design and color guidance

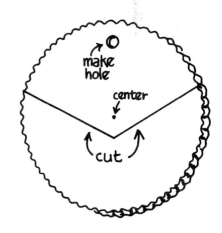

Ruffled Fan Ornament

Tint half the dough yellow and roll it out to ³⁄₁₆″ thick. Cut a circle with the scalloped cookie cutter and cut the circle into a fan as shown in the diagram below right. Use the blunt end of the wooden skewer to make a hanging hole large enough for the ribbon to fit through.

Allow the fan to dry, turning it over occasionally so it dries evenly.

When the fan is dry, turn it wrong side up and glue the lace to the top edge. Trim the excess lace. When the glue has dried slightly, turn the fan right side up; the weight of the fan will keep the lace in position while the glue dries.

Meanwhile, make the decorations: Break off small pieces of dough and color them orange, green, blue and lavender. Reserve a bit of white dough; color the remaining dough pink. Roll out the pink to ¹⁄₁₆″ to ⅛″ and cut a strip ¼″ wide and 6½″ long. Shape it into a bow as shown below, using a bit of water to secure the strip in the center and when you wrap a short strip around the center.

Roll out pink, orange and lavender dough to ¹⁄₁₆″ thick and cut a flower from each. Roll six small blue balls and flatten them into disks. Roll three tiny white balls. With the green dough, make six little leaves (rolled ovals and flattened ovals) and two curved stems. Roll 16 to 18 small pink balls. Set the decorations aside to dry on waxed paper.

When all the parts are dry, glue the decorations in place, following the photograph. Use the tweezers to pick up each piece, dip it in glue and place it on the fan. Let the glue dry thoroughly.

Hang the ornament with narrow satin ribbon.

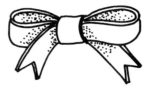

Round Ruffled Ornament

You will need:

Small amount of sugar paste dough

Food coloring

Rolling pin

Scalloped round cookie cutter, 3″ in diameter

Plastic straw

Lace ruffle, ¾″ wide and 16″ long

Needle and thread

Silver beads

White glue

Satin ribbon, ⅛″ wide

Adjoining photograph for design and color guidance

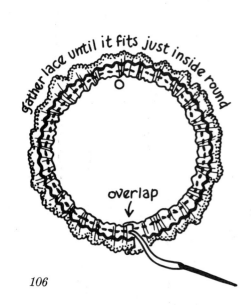

Round Ruffled Ornament

Roll some white dough to ³⁄₁₆″ to ¼″ thick. Use the cookie cutter to cut a round and then use the plastic straw to make a hole in the round. Set the round aside to dry on waxed paper, turning it over occasionally so that it dries evenly.

Meanwhile, make the roses and leaves: Color two small pieces of dough for the roses; I used blue and lavender but you might prefer pink, yellow and/or peach. Make a two-petal rose for the center of the ornament and six or seven rosebuds to surround it (making some in each color of dough); see page 33 for instructions on making roses and buds. Cut off the bottom of the rose and four buds at an angle.

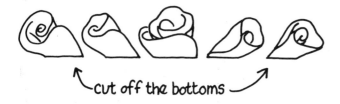

cut off the bottoms

Color a small piece of dough green for the leaves. For each leaf, roll a narrow oval and flatten it to be very thin and delicate. Make ten or twelve leaves. Set the roses and leaves aside to dry on waxed paper.

When the white round is dry, make the ruffle for the edge: Cut a piece of lace ruffle 1½″ times the circumference of the round. With needle and thread, gather the lace until it fits just inside the round, as shown. Overlap and stitch the ends, spread the gathers evenly and iron lightly to set the gathers in place. Turn the white round wrong side up and put glue along the edge. Lay the ruffle over the glue and press gently in position. When the glue has dried slightly, turn the ornament right side up; the weight of the round will keep the lace in position while the glue dries.

When the glue is dry, decorate the ornament: Glue the rosebuds in a pretty arrangement with the two-petal rose in the center, using the photograph as a guide for placement. Glue nine or ten leaves around the rosebuds, tucking one leaf in the center. Glue silver beads around the edge, one at each scallop. Allow the glue to dry thoroughly.

Hang the ornament with two pieces of satin ribbon.

gather lace until it fits just inside round

overlap

Petals-and-Pearls Ornament

You will need:

Small amount of sugar paste dough

Food coloring

Rolling pin

Cookie cutters: three flower-shaped cutters in graduated sizes (small, medium, large)

Plastic straw

Pearl beads

White glue

Narrow ribbon

Adjoining photograph for design and color guidance

Petals-and-Pearls Ornament

Divide the dough in three parts. Tint each part a different color. Roll out one piece of dough to ⅛″ thick and cut out the large flower. Use the plastic straw to cut a hanging hole in one petal. Roll out the second piece of dough and cut out the medium-size flower. Roll out the third piece of dough and cut out the small flower. Set the flowers on waxed paper to dry, turning them over occasionally so they dry evenly.

When they are dry, glue the flowers together as in the photograph and glue a few pearl beads to the center of the top flower.

Hang the ornament with narrow ribbon.

Here are some color suggestions, the first in each group being the color of the smallest flower: bright yellow, pale yellow, grass green; light pink, dark pink, lavender; pale blue, blue, lavender; yellow, peach, orange; white, pale pink, pink.

Diamond Ornament

You will need:

Small amount of sugar paste dough

Food coloring

Rolling pin

Diamond-shaped cookie cutter

Plastic straw

Flat gold trim

White glue, tweezers

Gold cord

Adjoining photograph for design and color guidance

Diamond Ornament

Break off two-thirds of the dough and tint it peach (or any color you prefer). Roll the dough out to ⅛″ thick and cut a diamond. Trim off the side points of the diamond and make a hanging hole in the top point with the plastic straw. Set the diamond aside to dry on waxed paper, turning it over occasionally so it dries evenly.

When it is dry, turn the diamond wrong side up and apply the gold trim: Cut one piece of gold trim for each edge. Apply glue to the edge of the

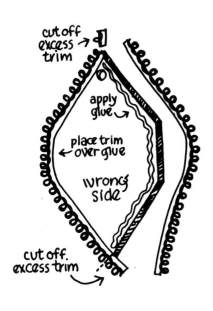

cut off excess trim

apply glue →

place trim over glue ←

wrong side

cut off. excess trim

ornament and place the trim over the glue. Allow the glue to dry and then snip off the excess gold trim.

Meanwhile, make the decorations for the diamond: Color a small piece of dough blue (or any color you prefer) and roll 30 to 35 "rice kernels." Roll 20 to 25 tiny balls using the remaining white dough. Let all the decorations dry.

Glue the decorations to the diamond, following the photograph for placement; use tweezers to pick up each piece, dip it in glue and place it in position on the ornament. Allow the glue to dry.

Hang the ornament with gold cord.

Snowflake Ornaments

You will need:

½ recipe of flour/salt dough
Rolling pin
Cookie cutters: round, about 2½″ in diameter; round, about 3½″ in diameter
Assortment of aspic cutters
Wooden skewer

Acrylic paints, brushes
Polyurethane, turpentine
Silver glitter
Narrow ribbon

Drawings, page 109, for design and color guidance

The basic method is simple: Roll dough out to ¼″ thick and cut a large or small round with one of the cookie cutters. Use the aspic cutters to cut designs in the round and to cut pieces to add around the edge (attach the pieces with water). Then use the blunt end of the skewer to make a hole large enough to accommodate the ribbon for hanging the ornament. Transfer the snowflake to a flour-dusted cookie sheet, bake it at low heat until hard and remove it from the oven to cool. Paint the snowflake white, allow the paint to dry and then paint it a pretty pastel. When the paint is dry, brush the ornament with polyurethane and sprinkle it with glitter. Tap off the excess glitter, let the polyurethane dry and then brush on several more coats of polyurethane, allowing each coat to dry before brushing on the next.

Hang the snowflake with narrow ribbon.

The drawing on the opposite page shows four designs for snowflakes and indicates which aspic cutter shapes to cut out or add for each. Feel free to invent your own designs, utilizing whatever cutters you like best.

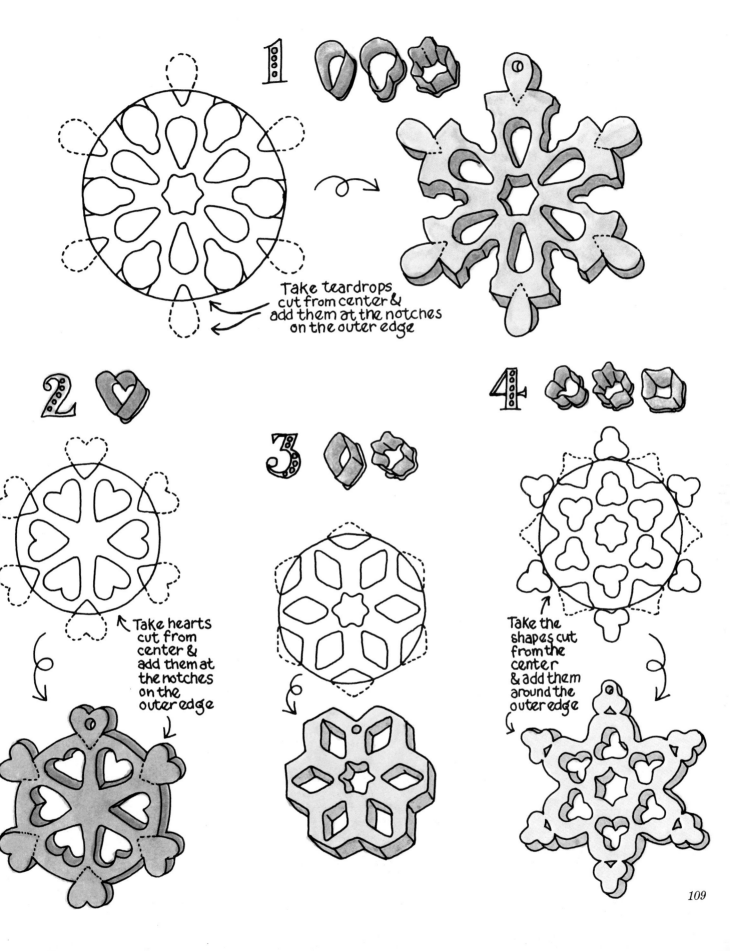

1

Take teardrops cut from center & add them at the notches on the outer edge

2

Take hearts cut from center & add them at the notches on the outer edge

3

4

Take the shapes cut from the center & add them around the outer edge

Gingerbread House

You will need for the base:

2 pieces of foam core, each
   12″ x 16″
White glue
Gold (or other) ribbon, ½″ wide and
   2 yards long

You will need for the house:

1 recipe of gingerbread dough
2 heavy-duty cookie sheets
Thin cardboard for making
   patterns *or* a ruler and triangle
Sharp knife
Cookie cutters: small heart, 1¼″
   across; scalloped round, 1½″ in
   diameter; Christmas tree

You will need for the decoration:

2 recipes of decorating icing
Food coloring (green and yellow)
2 pastry bags
2 icing tips, one small round and
   one medium round
Palette knife, small spatula
Candies: party cinnamons (round
   red drops); cinnamon imperials
   (multi-color drops); twelve
   small candy canes; raspberry-
   shaped candies; small pillow-
   shaped hard candies (stripes
   and solid colors); green crystal
   sugar

*Photograph, below, for design
and color guidance*

Gingerbread House with Gingerbread Folks, pages 116 and 117

MAKING THE BASE

Glue the two pieces of foam core together and weight them with books while the glue dries. Glue the gold ribbon around the edge of the base; trim off any excess ribbon.

MAKING AND BAKING THE PIECES OF THE HOUSE AND THE TREES

The pieces you need for the house are shown in the diagram below. Cut thin cardboard to the right measurements to make patterns or plan to use a ruler and triangle to cut the pieces directly on the rolled-out dough.

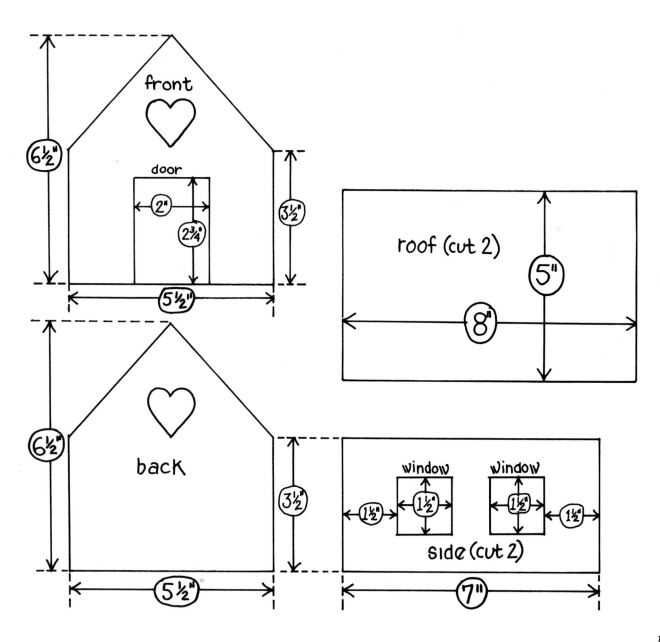

Dust the backs of the cookie sheets with flour and roll out dough on each sheet to about ³⁄₁₆″ to ¼″ thick. Cut out the front and back on one cookie sheet and the two sides on the other cookie sheet. Remove the excess dough. Be sure to leave space between the pieces because the dough spreads during baking. Follow these additional instructions as well:

Front: Cut out a heart (use the cookie cutter) and a door (use a ruler and sharp knife) as indicated in the diagram on the preceding page. Discard the heart but save and bake the door.

Back: Cut out a heart as indicated in the diagram.

Sides: Cut out windows (with ruler and sharp knife) as in the diagram.

Set the leftover dough aside to reuse. Bake these pieces according to the recipe. Remove them from the oven, run a long spatula under the pieces to loosen them while the cookie sheet is still hot, then allow the pieces to cool before taking them off the cookie sheets.

Knead the leftover dough together. Dust the back of one cookie sheet with flour again and roll dough out on that sheet, to ³⁄₁₆″ to ¼″ thick. Cut out the roof pieces on this cookie sheet, according to the measurements on the diagram. Remove the excess dough.

Roll leftover dough to ³⁄₁₆″ to ¼″ thick on flour-dusted surface (not cookie sheet). Cut out eight Christmas trees and one wreath (the wreath is cut with the scalloped round; cut a smaller round out of the center). Roll the remaining dough to ⅛″ thick and cut out 50 hearts. Transfer the trees, wreath and hearts to the second cookie sheet.

Bake the roof pieces and the cookies according to the recipe. Remove them from the oven, run a spatula under them to loosen them, then allow them to cool. Take all the pieces off the cookie sheets except 25 of the hearts. Return those 25 hearts to the oven to get very brown. When they have browned sufficiently (see close-up photograph of Gingerbread House), remove them from the oven and allow them to cool.

DECORATING THE INDIVIDUAL PIECES

Put half of one recipe of icing in a separate bowl and color it with green and a little yellow food coloring to make bright green. Fill one pastry bag with green icing and attach the small round tip. Fill the other pastry bag with white icing and attach the medium round tip.

Roof pieces: Lay out the hearts on the roof pieces, alternating light and dark hearts, as in the photograph on page 110. You'll have hearts left over. Lift each heart, pipe a little white icing on the back and replace the heart. Pipe dots of white icing between the hearts and place a party cinnamon on each dot. The icing dries quickly so pipe only three or four dots at a time.

Side pieces: Break eight candy canes as shown below; use the short straight pieces on the window and reserve the curved pieces for the fence. Break four more candy canes as shown; use the long straight pieces on the windows and discard the leftovers. Pipe white icing around each window; place one short piece of candy cane on each side, one long piece across the top and several peppermint-striped hard candies along the bottom.

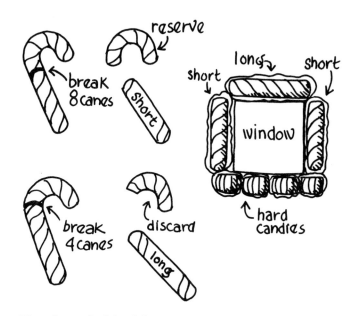

Back: Pipe a line of white icing around the heart. Pipe dots of white icing around the line and place a cinnamon imperial on each dot. Pipe scallops of green icing along the top edges.

Front: Repeat as above. Then pipe large white dots around the door, a few at a time, and cover each with a peppermint-striped hard candy.

Door and wreath: Pipe some white icing on the back of the wreath and place it on the door. Pipe green icing all over the wreath in a squiggly pattern and stud it with party cinnamons.

Trees: If the trees have trunks, carefully score each one with a damp knife and break off the trunk. Pipe green loops in rows across each tree, starting at the bottom. After piping a couple of rows, stop and sprinkle the icing with green crystal sugar. Tap off the excess sugar and go on to pipe the next two rows. Press party cinnamons on the completed trees.

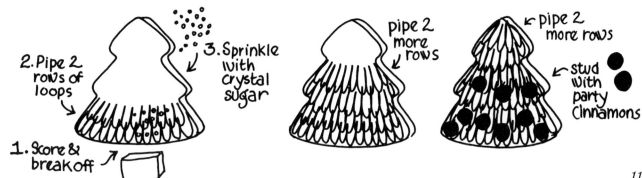

pipe icing on the back

Allow the icing on all the pieces to dry for about half an hour. When the icing has hardened, pipe some white icing on the backs of two trees and place the trees on the back piece, even with the lower edge. Let the icing dry.

PUTTING THE PIECES TOGETHER

Draw a rectangle 5½" x 7" on the base, as in the diagram below. Pipe a fat line of white icing just outside the pencil line that indicates the back and one side. Place the back piece on the line of icing and then pipe icing along the edge of the back piece. Place the side piece in position on the line of icing, pressing against the back piece. Hold the two pieces together with one hand and pipe more icing along the joint inside and outside the house and along the base line. Hold the pieces in place until they can stand by themselves. Allow the icing to dry for a few minutes.

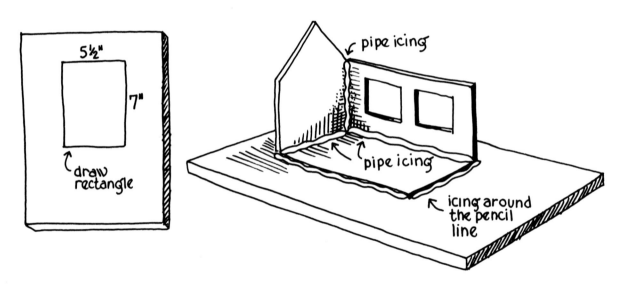

5½"

7"

draw rectangle

pipe icing

pipe icing

icing around the pencil line

Repeat this process to attach the other side piece and the front piece. Let the icing dry for half an hour.

Attach the roof pieces one at a time: Pipe white icing on three edges as shown in the diagram and place the roof gently in position on the icing; it should overhang the side but be even with the peak of the roof. Hold it

icing on three edges

114

lightly—without pressing—in position for a minute or two until the icing hardens enough to hold the roof piece on. Reinforce it by piping more icing at the front and back joints inside and outside the house and at the side joint inside. Let the icing dry for half an hour.

Repeat this process for the second roof piece, reinforcing it on the outside of the house, front and back, and along the peak of the roof.

Pipe white icing on one long edge of the door opening and gently press the door in place, as shown in the photograph.

FINISHING THE HOUSE

With the pastry bag and the small spatula or palette knife, pipe and spread icing about ½″ thick in the doorway and the path area *only*. Put hard candies in place for the path and edge the path with the curved pieces of candy cane you set aside earlier.

Continue to spread icing around the front of the house. Pipe white icing on the backs of two trees and press them in position against the front of the house. Spread icing at least ½″ thick all the way to the front edge of the base. Imbed a tree near each front corner of the base, as shown in the photograph. Pipe icing around the base of each tree, if necessary, to make it stand up straight. Stud the front yard with a few raspberry-shaped candies.

Spread icing along one side of the house all the way to the edge of the base and press raspberry-shaped candies along the base line. Repeat this procedure on the other side of the house. Spread icing around the back of the house, right to the back of the base, and imbed a tree near each corner. Pipe icing around the base of each tree, if necessary, to make it stand up straight.

Finally, add the roofline decorations: Pipe large white dots, a few at a time, along the point of the roof, the front edges and the back edges. Stud each dot with a party cinnamon. Let the icing dry overnight.

Gingerbread Folks, page 117
Star/Bell/Candy Cane Garland #2, page 118
Cookie Wreath, page 119

Gingerbread Folks

You will need:

1 recipe (or more) of gingerbread
   dough
Cookie cutters: gingerbread boy;
   gingerbread girl
1 recipe of decorating icing
Food coloring

Pastry bags
Icing tips, one round and one star

*Photograph, page 116, for design
   and color guidance*

Roll out the gingerbread dough to ⅛″ to ¼″ thick and cut out the boys and girls. Bake the cookies according to the recipe and allow them to cool while you prepare the icing. Divide the icing into four parts, each in its own bowl, and color one part pink, one part green and one part yellow, leaving one part white. Cover tightly with plastic wrap. Prepare the pastry bags by filling each one half full of icing as described in Chapter 1.

The following diagram shows the design and the tips used for the cookies.

Pink = round tip
Blue = star tip
Light brown = cookie

The first thing to do is to outline each cookie and draw the waistline, using the round tip. Outline several in white, then move the round tip to the pink icing bag and outline several in pink, then yellow, then green. Leaving the round tip on, go back and do some of the detail work. Move the tip back to a different color and continue with the detail work. Work with the round tip until you have done as much as you can with each color. Then change to the star tip and do the buttons, shoes, etc., working with each color in turn.

Let the icing dry until it is hard.

Star/Bell/Candy Cane Garland #2

You will need:

1 recipe of flour/salt dough
Red food coloring
Rolling pin
Cookie cutters: small star; small
  heart
Cookie sheet

Sharp knife
Wooden skewer
Polyurethane, turpentine, brush
Narrow ribbon
*Photograph, page 116, for design
  and color guidance*

MAKING THE STARS AND BELLS

Divide the dough in half; rewrap one half and set it aside for the candy canes. Use the remaining half for the stars and bells.

Roll out small amounts of dough to ⅛″ thick and cut out three stars or bells at a time. Make a stringing hole in each piece—make the hole immediately, before the dough forms a dry crust. Use the blunt end of a wooden skewer to make each hole, rotating the skewer in the hole to enlarge it. Turn each piece over, insert the skewer from the back and rotate it to make a clean hole. Make the hole larger in diameter than the ribbon since the hole will close up slightly during baking. Repeat the process to make an equal number of stars and bells. Transfer the stars and bells to a flour-dusted cookie sheet.

MAKING THE CANDY CANES

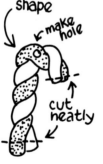

twist

shape

make hole

cut neatly

Divide the remaining dough in half and color one half pink with the red food coloring. For each cane, roll one pink strand 4½″ long and ¼″ in diameter and one natural-color strand 4½″ long and ¼″ in diameter. Twist the two strands together as shown. Place the twisted strands on the cookie sheet and shape into a candy cane. Cut the ends off neatly if necessary. Make three canes at a time and make a hole in each as described above.

BAKING, FINISHING AND STRINGING THE STARS, BELLS AND CANDY CANES

Bake the dough pieces at low heat until hard, watching carefully to be sure the pink dough does not brown. Remove from the oven and allow to cool. Brush each piece with a coat of sealer (a mixture of one-half polyurethane and one-half turpentine) and let the sealer dry thoroughly. Brush on several coats of polyurethane, letting each coat dry before applying the next. Be sure the stringing holes do not clog up with sealer or polyurethane.

Cut a piece of ribbon twice the width of your mantel and thread the end on a large needle. String on a star and tie a double knot to secure it. Skip three inches of ribbon, string a bell and tie a double knot. Skip three more inches, string a candy cane and tie a double knot. Repeat this sequence to the end of the ribbon.

Cookie Wreath

You will need:

1 recipe of flour/salt dough

Piece of sturdy paper at least 9″ square, e.g., a piece of a brown paper bag

Grease pencil or red crayon

Cookie sheet

Ruler

Sharp knife

Rolling pin

Cookie cutters: small five-petal flower; small heart; small eight-petal flower; aspic cutter star

Wooden skewer

Polyurethane, turpentine, brush

Epoxy glue

Adjoining photograph for design and color guidance

Cookie Wreath

MAKING THE FOUNDATION

The foundation looks like the first drawing in the sequence below. To make the foundation, first make a paper pattern. Cut the sturdy paper into a circle 9″ in diameter. Fold the circle in half, in quarters and then in eighths. Cut off the point of the folded circle along an arc 1½″ from the point—you have cut off a circle 3″ in diameter. Place the paper pattern on the back of the cookie sheet and use the grease pencil or crayon to outline it and mark the eighths. Connect the opposite points.

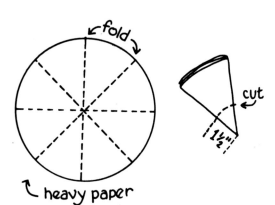

fold

cut

1½″

heavy paper

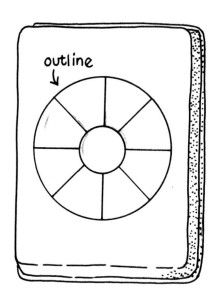

outline

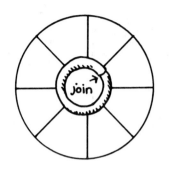

Dust the back of the cookie sheet with flour. Roll a strand of dough about 10″ long and ⅝″ in diameter. Shape the strand into a circle over the smaller crayonned circle and join the ends with water, cutting off any excess strand. Smooth out the joint.

Roll eight strands, each 8″ long and ⅝″ in diameter. Shape the strands to make the loops of the foundation, using the straight lines and the outline of the circle as guides for positioning. With a sharp knife, trim off the ends of each strand as you custom-fit it. Brush the ends with water and brush water between the loops to adhere them to the center circle and each other.

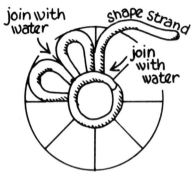

MAKING THE DECORATIONS

First decorate the foundation with rosebuds and leaves as shown in the photograph. For each rosebud, roll a thin strand of dough about 1″ long, flatten it and roll it up. Brush water on the bottom of the rosebud and press it into place on the foundation. Make as many rosebuds as needed to go all the way around the circle. Shape each leaf from a little ball of dough and incise a center line with the wooden skewer. Brush water on the underside of each leaf and press it into place on the circle. Make enough leaves to go all around the circle.

Next, make the flowers and heart-shaped leaves: Roll dough to ⅛″ thick. Use the five-petal cookie cutter to cut eight flowers; use the aspic cutter to incise a star in the center of each flower and the wooden skewer to incise the lines. Use the eight-petal cookie cutter to cut eight daisies; cut off the end of each petal and use the blunt end of the skewer to make the pattern in the center of the daisy. Use the heart cookie cutter to cut eight leaves; incise the center lines and veins on each leaf with the point of the skewer.

Transfer all the flowers and the leaves to the cookie sheet.

BAKING AND FINISHING THE WREATH

Bake the foundation and the decorations at low heat until hard. Remove from the oven and allow to cool. Lift the foundation from the cookie sheet and set it aside. Return the flowers and leaves to the oven to bake at a higher heat until they are a warm brown. Remove them from the oven and allow them to cool.

Brush a coat of sealer (a mixture of one-half polyurethane and one-half turpentine) on the foundation and on the decorations and let it dry thoroughly. Brush several coats of polyurethane on the foundation and decorations, allowing each coat to dry before applying the next.

Use epoxy to glue the decorations to the foundation in this order (using the photograph as a guide to placement): Glue the daisies to the loops; glue the leaves to the loops; glue the flowers to the loops *propped on the leaves*. Allow the glue to dry overnight.

How to Hang an Ornament

You will need:

Narrow ribbons in satin, grosgrain, velvet, taffeta

Inexpensive ribbons used for tying packages

Yarns in thick or thin weights, one or more strands

Plain round and flat cords

Fancy cords like soutache, middy braid, rat tail

Metallic gold, silver and bright-colored cords and braids

Baby rickrack

FOUR WAYS TO ATTACH THE RIBBON (CORD, YARN, ETC.)

1. Thread the ends of the ribbon through the hole and tie them in a bow. Trim the ends of the ribbon.

2. Slip a loop of ribbon through the hole, thread the ends of the ribbon through the loop and tie a bow or knot.

3. Glue the ends of the ribbon to the back of the ornament.

4. Thread one end of the ribbon through the hole and tie a bow.

TWO WAYS TO MAKE A HOLE

1. Press the end of a plastic straw all the way through the dough without lifting the dough. Withdraw the straw gently, taking the bit of dough out with it. If you need the straw to make more holes, be sure to pick out the dough with a toothpick.

2. Press the blunt end of a wooden skewer through the dough without lifting the dough. Make a tiny circular motion with the skewer to enlarge the hole as much as necessary. Be sure the hole is clean and goes all the way through the dough.

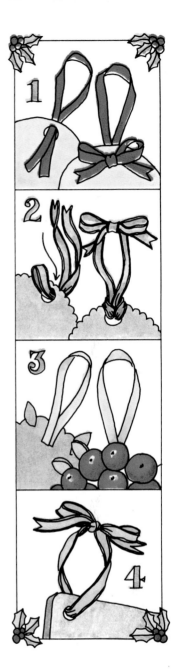

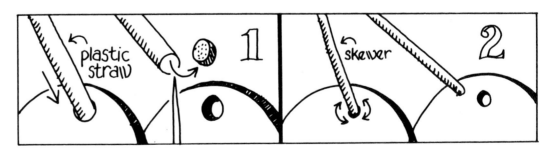

Thanksgiving, Valentine's Day and Easter

In this chapter, you'll find projects to help you celebrate these three holidays. If you take good care of the finished items and store them carefully, you'll be able to use them for years to come.

Important: Before you start, see which dough is specified in the "You will need" list at the beginning of each project and be sure to read all the general information about that dough in Chapter 1.

Turkey Place Card Holder, page 125
Kitten Napkin Rings, page 126

Turkey Place Card Holder

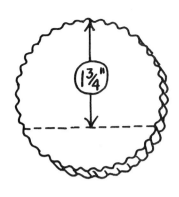

You will need:

1 recipe of flour/salt dough
Rolling pin
Cookie cutter: scalloped round,
    2½″ in diameter; smaller
    scalloped round, about 1½″ in
    diameter
Cookie sheet

Wooden skewer
Knife or spatula
Acrylic paints, brushes
Polyurethane, turpentine

*Photograph, page 124, for design
and color guidance*

Note: The instructions given below are for making one bird, but you can make several at a time.

Start by making the tail of the bird. Roll dough to ⅛″ thick. Use the larger cookie cutter to cut out a round and then cut off the lower part of the round. Use the smaller cookie cutter to make a deep impression in the round. Be careful not to press the smaller cutter all the way through the round. Incise the lines on the tail with a wooden skewer.

incise lines   make impression with small cutter

Place the round on a flour-dusted cookie sheet.

Next make the body. Roll a ball of dough into an egg shape, about 1″ in diameter. Place it on the cookie sheet. Roll a smaller, longer egg shape for the neck and adhere it to the body with a bit of water. With a knife or spatula, cut a deep gash in the top of the body—don't cut all the way through!

Bake the pieces at low heat for about half an hour, until partially hardened. Remove the cookie sheet from the oven.

While the pieces are still very warm, brush them with water, place a little ball of unbaked dough between them and press them together firmly. Brush water on the neck and add a small pointed oval for the head. Decorate the back of the turkey with small ovals and small balls as shown.

Return the turkey to the oven and bake at low heat until completely hard. Remove from the oven and cool.

Paint the turkey white and when the white paint is dry, paint it as you see in the photograph. Allow the paint to dry thoroughly and then brush on several coats of polyurethane. Let each coat of polyurethane dry before applying the next.

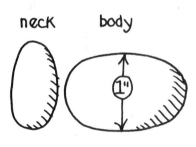

neck   body

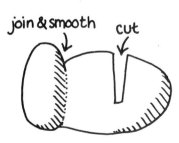

join & smooth   cut

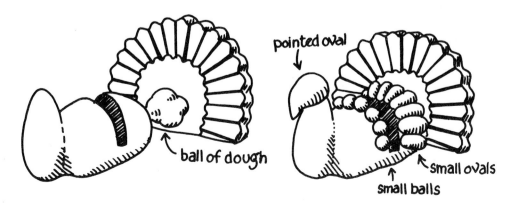

pointed oval

ball of dough

small ovals

small balls

Kitten Napkin Rings

You will need:

Small amount of flour/salt dough
Wooden napkin rings with flat
   sides

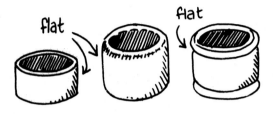

Rolling pin

Cookie cutters: small kitten; plain
   round just large enough to
   accommodate the kitten (see
   photo, page 124, for
   relationship)
Cookie sheet
Acrylic paint (burnt sienna),
   brushes
Small piece of sandpaper
Polyurethane, turpentine
Epoxy glue

*Photograph, page 124, for design
and color guidance*

Roll out dough to ¼″ thick. Use the plain round to cut as many circles as you have napkin rings. Cut an equal number of kittens. Brush the back of each kitten with water and center it on a circle. Use a wooden skewer or toothpick to incise the face and tail.

Transfer the circles to a cookie sheet. Bake the circles at low heat until hard. Remove from the oven and allow to cool.

Mix a little burnt sienna paint with water to make a thin wash. Paint the wash on the circle but *not* on the kitten. When the paint is completely dry, brush on a coat of sealer (a mixture of one-half turpentine and one-half polyurethane). Let the sealer dry.

Sand a narrow strip on each napkin ring where the circle will be glued. Use epoxy to glue each circle to a napkin ring. Let the epoxy dry completely and then brush several coats of polyurethane on each circle and napkin ring, allowing each coat to dry before applying the next.

Lovebirds Wall Piece, page 128

Lovebirds Wall Piece

You will need:

1 recipe of flour/salt dough
Rolling pin
Small heart cookie cutter, about
    1½″ across
Tracing paper, carbon paper and
    thin cardboard for making a
    pattern
Sharp knife, ruler

Cookie sheet
11 finishing nails, 1½″ long
Aluminum foil
Polyurethane, turpentine, brushes

*Photograph, page 127, for design
    and color guidance*

MAKING THE LOVEBIRDS AND HEARTS

Trace the lovebird pattern, transfer it to thin cardboard and cut it out (see page 18 for instructions on making and using patterns). Roll some dough out to ¼″ thick. Use the pattern to cut two lovebirds from the rolled dough— one facing left and one facing right. Incise the lines on wings and tails with a sharp knife; make the eyes with a toothpick. Set the birds aside for now. Use the heart cookie cutter to cut out five hearts.

MAKING THE FRAME FOR THE BIRDS

Center the birds at one end of the flour-dusted back of a cookie sheet, noses touching as in the photograph. Roll a strand of dough about ½″ in diameter and 24″ long. Shape the strand around the birds on the cookie sheet, lifting the tails onto the strand. Flatten the strand where the tails overlap it and flatten the ends of the strand before tucking them under the heads of the birds. Brush water between the strand and the birds at the overlaps.

Roll another strand ½″ in diameter and 8″ long, two strands each ½″ in diameter and 6″ long and a fourth strand ½″ in diameter and 7″ long. Shape the strands into loops as shown in the diagram, flattening the ends and brushing them with water before tucking them under. *Note:* Be sure the loops are generous enough to accommodate your hearts.

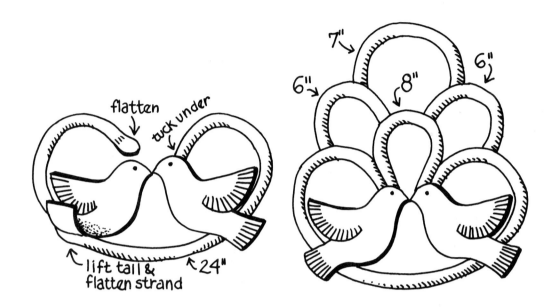

ADDING THE HEARTS AND BALLS

Insert nails about ¾″ deep in the hearts as shown in the photograph. Place each heart in position on the cookie sheet and gently pull the nails out to pierce the strands. Nails are correctly positioned when they are inserted equally in the hearts and the strands.

Roll small balls to decorate the loops. Brush water on the loops and between the balls as you place them in position.

BAKING AND FINISHING THE WALL PIECE

Prop up the tails of the birds with crumpled aluminum foil. Bake the wall piece at low heat until it is hard and nicely browned. About halfway through the baking, run a long spatula under the piece to loosen it from the baking sheet.

Remove the piece from the oven and allow it to cool. Brush it with a coat of sealer (a mixture of one-half polyurethane and one-half turpentine) and let the sealer dry thoroughly. Then brush on several coats of polyurethane, letting each coat dry before applying the next.

Valentine Card with Ornament, page 131
Valentine Cookies, page 132

Valentine Card with Ornament

You will need:

Small amount of bread/glue dough

Food coloring

Rolling pin

Cookie cutters: small heart;
   flower-shaped aspic cutter

Wooden skewer

Blank card and envelope

White glue

Narrow ribbon

*Photograph, page 130, for design
and color guidance*

Color a small piece of dough red and the rest of the dough pink. Roll the pink dough out to ⅛″ thick and use the heart cookie cutter to cut six hearts. Place the hearts on a piece of waxed paper and arrange them in a circle, touching each other at the sides. Brush water sparingly at the points of contact and press the hearts firmly together. Be sure they stick to each other. Use the blunt end of a wooden skewer to make two holes at the top of one heart; the holes must be large enough to allow the ribbon to pass through.

Roll the red dough out very thin and use the aspic cutter to cut six flowers. Brush the back of each flower with water and press it in position on a heart, following the photograph for placement. Allow the ornament to dry completely. When it is dry, slip the ends of the ribbon through the holes and tie a bow.

Put a few dabs of white glue on the back of the ornament and press it in position on the blank card. Allow the glue to dry. After Valentine's Day, the ornament can be removed and hung on the wall or saved for the Christmas tree.

Valentine Cookies

You will need:

1 recipe (or more) of cookie dough
Cookie cutters: small heart;
    medium heart; large heart;
    medium flower; small round,
    about 1″ in diameter, with or
    without scalloped edge

1 recipe of decorating icing
Food coloring
Pastry bags
Icing tips, one round and one star

*Photograph, page 130, for
    additional design and color
    guidance*

Roll out the dough and cut out hearts and flowers. *Note:* As you can see in the photograph, some of the cookies are layered. For example, the flowers have small rounds on their centers and some of the medium-sized hearts have smaller hearts centered on them. Be sure to cut enough cookies for any layering you may wish to do, e.g., cutting one small round cookie for the center of each flower you cut.

Bake the cookies according to the recipe and let them cool while you prepare one batch of decorating icing. Divide the icing into small bowls and tint each a different color—pink, blue, lavender, yellow, green. Make as many colors as you like but be sure to keep one bowl white. Cover the bowls tightly with plastic wrap. Prepare the pastry bags by filling each half full of icing as described in Chapter 1. Attach the round tip to one bag and the star tip to another bag. Decorate the cookies.

When you cut the cookies and later when you begin to decorate them, follow the photo for design inspiration or invent your own designs. The diagrams will show you which icing tips to use for some of my designs.

Tip: Do as much decorating as you can with each icing tip and icing color before switching to the next. For example, couple the star tip to the bag of pink icing. First pipe the star borders on several medium-sized hearts, then the pink flowers on the large hearts and then the outlines of the petals on the flower cookies. Continue in this way with each color, alternating the tips. There will be some backtracking as you complete your designs but you'll keep it to a minimum if you use this technique.

Allow the icing to dry before serving the cookies.

Pink = round tip
Blue = star tip
Light brown = cookie

Checkerboard Heart, page 135
Cupid-with-Hearts and Braided Heart, page 136

Checkerboard Heart Ornament

You will need:

Small amount of flour/salt dough
Rolling pin
Round cookie cutter, 1½″ to 2½″ in
    diameter
Sharp knife, ruler

Paper clip, wire cutter
Cookie sheet
Polyurethane, turpentine, brush
Ribbon
*Photograph, page 134, for design
    and color guidance*

The size of this heart is based on the diameter of the round cookie cutter.
Roll the dough to ¼″ thick and make the heart like this:

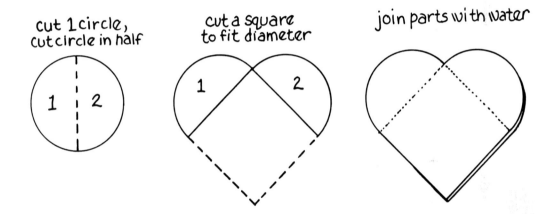

cut 1 circle,
cut circle in half

cut a square
to fit diameter

join parts with water

Use a spatula to transfer the heart to a flour-dusted cookie sheet.

Roll some dough to 1″ thick. Cut eleven little squares as shown and adhere
them to the heart with water. Cut off the excess dough at the edge of the
heart. With the wire cutters, snip a U-shaped hanger from a paper clip and
insert it at the top of the heart.

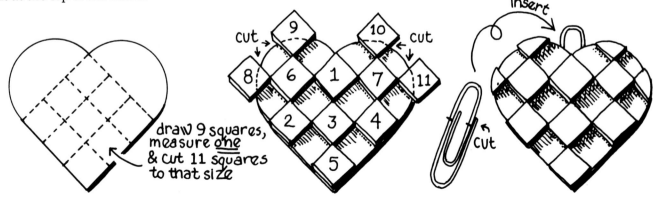

draw 9 squares,
measure one
& cut 11 squares
to that size

cut

cut

insert

cut

Transfer the heart to a flour-dusted cookie sheet. Bake the heart at low
heat until hard and lightly browned. Do not turn it over during baking.
Remove it from the oven and let it cool. Brush with a coat of sealer and,
when the sealer is dry, with several coats of polyurethane. Allow each coat
to dry before applying the next. Hang with ribbon.

135

Cupid-with-Hearts Ornament

You will need:

Small amount of flour/salt dough

Rolling pin

Cookie cutters: gingerbread boy; small heart

Garlic press

Wooden skewer

Paper clip, wire cutter

Cookie sheet

Acrylic paints (white and red), brushes

Polyurethane, turpentine

Ribbon

Photograph, page 134, for design and color guidance

Roll the dough out to ¼″ thick. With the cookie cutters, cut out one gingerbread boy and two small hearts. Bend the boy's arms and legs into the position you see in the photo, perching the hearts firmly on his hands with a drop or two of water. Force a bit of dough through the garlic press. Brush Cupid's head with water and apply the squiggly strands for hair. Incise the face with the blunt and pointed ends of the wooden skewer—and don't forget the belly button! Use the wire cutters to snip a U-shaped hanger from a paper clip and insert the hanger at the top of Cupid's head. Transfer Cupid to a flour-dusted cookie sheet.

Bake the ornament at low heat until hard. Remove it from the oven and allow it to cool. Paint *only* the hearts white and then red. When the paint is dry, paint a coat of sealer *only* on Cupid. When the sealer is dry, brush several coats of polyurethane on the entire ornament, allowing each coat to dry thoroughly before applying the next. Hang the ornament with ribbon.

Braided Heart Ornament

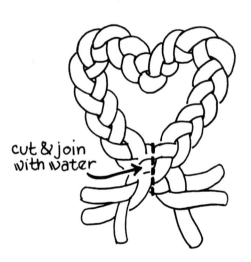

cut & join
with water

You will need:

Small amount of flour/salt dough

Cookie sheet

Sharp knife

Polyurethane, turpentine, brush

Ribbon

Photograph, page 134, for design and color guidance

Divide the dough into three parts and roll each part to a long strand. Braid the strands on a flour-dusted cookie sheet, working from the center out to both ends, to make a piece 12″ long. Shape the braid into a heart, miter the point with a sharp knife (cutting off any excess braid) and join the two ends with a bit of water. Bake at low heat without turning until hard and lightly browned. Remove from the oven and allow to cool.

Brush the heart with a coat of sealer and then with several coats of polyurethane, letting each coat dry before applying the next. Glue a loop of ribbon to the back of the heart.

Heart-Shaped Box, below
Valentine Basket with Hearts, page 140
Valentine Basket with Roses, page 141

Heart-Shaped Box

You will need:

1 recipe of sugar paste dough

Food coloring

Rolling pin

Cookie cutters: large heart about
    4¼″ across at the widest part;
    small bird

Ruler, sharp knife

Pastry cutter

White glue

Tweezers, toothpicks

*Photograph, above, for design and
    color guidance*

Note: Familiarize yourself with Technique #3 on page 31 and the instructions for making roses on page 33 of Chapter 1.

MAKING THE BASIC BOX

Break off two-thirds of the dough and color it pink. Roll a portion of the pink dough into a thick strand. With a rolling pin, flatten the strand so you have a long strip. Cut the edges of the strip straight and parallel, making the strip as wide as the heart cookie cutter is high. Wrap the strip around the heart, cutting off the excess at the point of the heart. Wet the ends of the strip at the point and pinch them together. Allow the strip to dry on the cookie cutter.

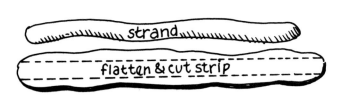

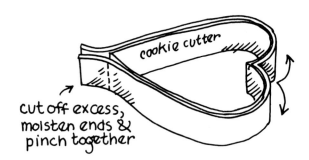

When the strip is dry, remove it very carefully from the cookie cutter. Roll out the remaining pink dough to ⅛″ thick. Place the dry heart-shaped strip on the rolled dough and cut around it with the pastry cutter about ¼″ from the strip to make a flat heart-shaped piece. Repeat to make a second flat heart-shaped piece. Allow both pieces to dry, turning them occasionally so they dry evenly. One will be the bottom of the box and the other will be the lid.

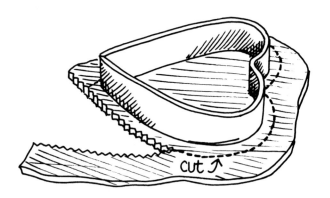

MAKING THE LID

Center the heart-shaped strip on the wrong side (the less perfect side) of one of the flat hearts. Make a light pencil line on the flat heart (the lid) around the inside of the heart-shaped strip. Remove the strip. Roll a strand about ⅛″ in diameter and 18″ long. Brush water on the lid about ⅛″ inside the pencil line and place the strand on the water. Press gently to adhere the strand and cut off any excess strand at the point of the heart. Allow the dough to dry.

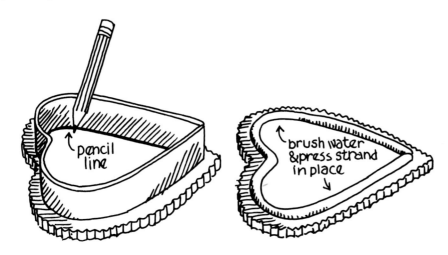

FINISHING THE BOTTOM OF THE BOX

Spread white glue on the bottom edge of the heart-shaped strip and center it on the other flat heart. Allow the glue to dry thoroughly.

MAKING THE PARTS OF THE DECORATIONS

Make all the parts, set them aside to dry on waxed paper and then arrange them on the lid to see how the design works out. (You may have to make additional pieces or eliminate some of the ones you made, depending on the size of your heart box.)

Divide the remaining dough and color small pieces of it dark pink, blue, green and lavender and keep some of it uncolored. You should have a bit of light pink left from making the box and you will need a tiny bit of orange.

Bow: Roll the dark pink dough out to a long thin rectangle. Cut a strip ¼" wide and 6" long and fold it to make a bow. Trim off the excess by notching the ends of the bow. Wrap a short length of strip around the center of the bow.

Birds: Roll the uncolored dough out to ⅛" thick and use the cookie cutter to cut two birds. Model the wings by hand and attach them with a bit of water, following the photograph for placement. Roll orange eyes and attach them, too.

Roses: Make three small roses according to the directions on page 33 in Chapter 1. Two petals per rose will be enough. Don't forget to cut the bottoms flat.

Leaves: Make 10 to 12 small leaves. Each leaf is an oval rolled between your fingers and then flattened. Incise a center line on each leaf with a sharp knife blade.

Balls: Roll enough small blue balls to encircle each rose and enough small lavender balls to make a border.

PUTTING THE PARTS TOGETHER

When all the parts are completely dry and you have tested the design (using the photograph as a guide for placement), glue the decorations to the lid. *Tip:* Pick up each small piece with tweezers, dip it in glue and put it in position. Apply glue to the backs of the larger pieces and put them in place by hand. Allow the glue to dry.

Valentine Basket with Hearts

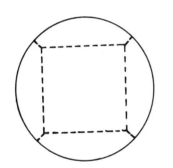

You will need:

½ recipe of sugar paste dough
Food coloring
Rolling pin
Cookie cutters: round with
  scalloped edge, about 4" in
  diameter; small heart

White glue
Tweezers, toothpicks

*Photograph, page 137, for design
and color guidance*

MAKING THE BASIC BASKET

Break off half the dough and color it pink. Roll the dough to ⅛" thick and use the scalloped cutter to cut out a circle. Working quickly, fold up the circle to form a square bottom, brush water in the corners and pinch them so the basket holds its shape. Allow the basket to dry.

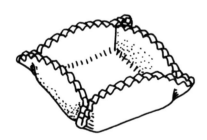

MAKING THE DECORATIONS

Of the remaining uncolored dough, color a small amount dark pink, a small amount green and a tiny amount blue. Leave the rest uncolored.

Roll out the dark pink dough to less than ⅛" thick and cut out four small hearts. For the flower petals, roll about 30 tiny white ovals and/or balls. Roll about ten oval or flattened oval green leaves. Roll a tiny blue ball for the center of each flower. Roll 15 to 20 small green balls for the edge decoration. Set all the parts aside to dry on waxed paper.

GLUING THE DECORATIONS TO THE BASKET

First glue each heart to a corner of the basket, as in the photograph. Then use tweezers to dip each petal, leaf and ball in white glue and put it in position on a heart or on the edge of the basket; follow the photograph for placement. Allow the glue to dry thoroughly before using the basket.

Valentine Basket with Roses

You will need:

½ recipe of sugar paste dough
Food coloring
Rolling pin
Round cookie cutter with
   scalloped edge, 4" in diameter,
   or any saucer, bowl or plate
   with a 4" diameter

Small jar, 1¼" to 1½" in diameter
White glue
Tweezers, toothpicks

*Photograph, page 137, for design
   and color guidance*

Reminder: Keep unused dough wrapped tightly at all times.

MAKING THE BASIC BASKET

Break off half the dough and color it lavender. Roll it out to less than ⅛" thick and cut out a circle 4" in diameter. Working quickly, pick up the circle of dough and drape it—centered—over the bottom of the small jar. The edges of the circle will fall in folds around the jar. You may have to try this a couple of times to get an arrangement of folds that you like. Allow the dough to dry in place on the upended jar.

MAKING THE ROSEBUDS AND LEAVES

Of the remaining uncolored dough, tint a small amount yellow, a small amount green and leave the rest uncolored. Following the instructions on page 33, make about ten yellow rosebuds and ten white rosebuds. *Note:* Some of the buds should be made with two petals instead of just one; do not cut off the pointy ends of the buds. Set the buds aside to dry on waxed paper.

Make two kinds of leaves: flattened ovals and rolled (unflattened) ovals. You'll need about 20 leaves altogether. Let them dry thoroughly.

GLUING THE DECORATIONS ON THE BASKET

Remove the dry basket from the jar. Allow the inside of the basket to dry some more if necessary. When the basket is completely dry, use white glue to attach the rosebuds and leaves both inside and outside the folds of the basket. Pick up each bud or leaf with tweezers, dip it in glue and put it in position. Allow the glue to dry thoroughly before using the basket.

Easter Basket, page 143
Decorated Easter Eggs, page 145
Flower-Topped Box, page 146

Easter Basket

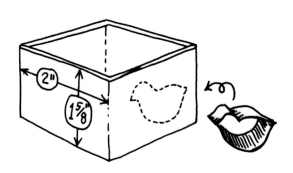

You will need:

1 recipe of sugar paste dough

Food coloring

Rolling pin

Cookie cutters: diamond with each of the four sides about 2″ long and the height about 1⅝″; small chick that fits on one side of the diamond; aspic cutter flower

Sharp knife

White glue

Tweezers, toothpicks

Photograph, page 142, for design and color guidance

Note: It is perfectly all right if your diamond is larger than the one specified. Also, if you do not have a chick and a flower, you may substitute other shapes and invent your own design to decorate the sides of the diamond.

MAKING THE BASIC BASKET

Measure one whole side (length and depth) of your diamond cookie cutter. Roll half of the dough to ⅛″ thick and cut two pieces of dough, each to those dimensions. Brush water on the ends of each piece and place a piece on each side of the diamond cookie cutter. Pinch the moistened ends together firmly where they meet, making sure they hold.

Allow the dough to dry until quite firm but not completely dry. Gently remove the cutter so the inside of the diamond shape can dry, too.

Knead the remaining dough into a smooth ball and roll it out to ⅛″ thick. Place the diamond shape on the rolled dough and carefully cut around it to make the bottom of the basket. Allow the bottom to dry, turning occasionally so it dries on both sides. Glue the diamond shape to the basket bottom and let the glue dry.

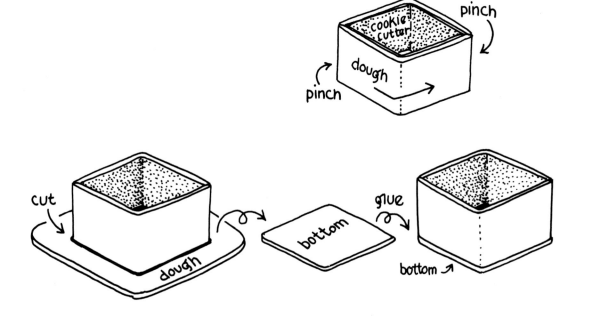

143

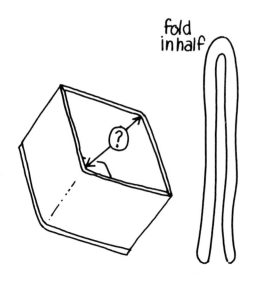

fold
in half

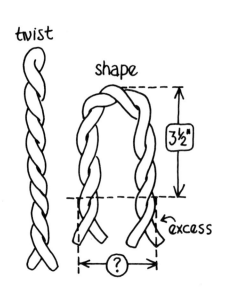

twist

shape

3½"

excess

?

To make the handle, measure the widest part of the diamond *inside* the basket. Roll a strand about 20″ long and ¼″ in diameter. Fold it in half and twist it. Lay the twist on waxed paper and curve it so it is about 3½″ high (cutting off any excess strand) and as wide at the bottom as the opening you measured. Allow the handle to dry completely.

MAKING THE DECORATIONS

While the basket is drying—and even before you make the handle—you can make the decorations and set them aside on waxed paper to dry.

Chicks: Break off a small piece of dough and color it yellow. Roll it to about ¹⁄₁₆″ thick and cut four chicks with the cookie cutter. Color a small piece of dough orange and roll four tiny balls for the eyes of the chicks. Adhere the eyes to the chicks with tiny dots of water.

Flowers: Break off a small piece of dough and color it lavender (or any other color you prefer). Roll the dough to ¹⁄₁₆″ thick and use the aspic cutter to cut 10 to 12 flowers.

Grass, stems and leaves: Break off a small piece of dough and color it grass green. Roll thin strands of dough and cut them into short pieces ranging in length from ⅜″ to ¾″. Make enough to go all the way around the bottom of the basket. The stems are thin strands cut slightly longer and then curved. The leaves are short curved pieces of thin strand with the ends rolled to points. Make about ten stems and ten leaves.

FINISHING THE BASKET

When all the decorations are dry, glue them to the basket, propping the basket up so you can work on one side at a time. Glue a chick, grass, stems, leaves and flowers on each side, using the photograph as a guide to placement. Note that the grass overlaps the lower edge of each chick. When the glue is thoroughly dry on one side, turn the basket to the next side and continue gluing the decorations on. Decorate all four sides.

Glue the handle in place, with the ends descending at least ½″ into the basket. While it dries, prop the handle up with a ball of crumpled waxed paper or tissue paper. Let it dry absolutely thoroughly before gently removing the crumpled paper.

Decorated Easter Eggs

You will need:

1 recipe of sugar paste dough
Hollow eggs
Food coloring
Rolling pin
Aspic cutters

Tweezers, toothpicks
White glue

*Photograph, page 142, for design
and color guidance*

Note: Read about sugar paste dough on pages 29 to 33 of Chapter 1, giving particular attention to the diagrams of sugar paste decorations (page 33).

Divide the dough into parts and tint each part a different color—light pink, dark pink, blue, orange, yellow, green, lavender, etc. Spend some time making a variety of tiny decorations in each color (balls, ovals, flattened rounds, flat petals, leaves, flowers and diamonds cut with aspic cutters). Set them all on waxed paper to dry. When they are dry, arrange the decorations in the designs shown in the photograph or make up designs of your own.

To apply the decorations, pick up each little piece with tweezers, dip it lightly in glue and place it in position on the egg. You may place several decorations in the same area at one time, but let the glue dry in each area before you try to turn the egg and decorate another section. Work on several eggs at the same time; move from egg to egg, finishing one area on each, and by the time you complete an area on the last egg, the first one will be ready to be turned.

Tip: Cover the holes on the ends of the eggs with little flattened rounds.

Flower-Topped Box

You will need:

1 recipe of sugar paste dough

Food coloring

Square box or jar made of glass, metal or plastic, about 3″ x 3″ and at least 2″ high, rounded at the bottom and with no bottom rim

Rolling pin

Sharp knife

Small bird cookie cutter (be sure it is smaller than the side of the jar)

White glue

Colored non-pareils (tiny candy dots)

Tweezers, toothpicks

Photograph, page 142, for design and color guidance

Note: Read the general information about sugar paste dough, pages 29 to 33 of Chapter 1, paying special attention to Technique #2.

MAKING THE BASIC BOX

You can use a square jar of any small size for the basic box. Just be sure to make accommodations in the decorations, e.g., adjusting the size of the bird and the flower.

Break off two-thirds of the dough and color it blue. *Reminder:* Keep any dough not in immediate use well wrapped in plastic. Roll the blue dough out to ⅛″ thick. Place the square jar in the center of the dough and cut the cross shape as shown in the diagram below. Work quickly! There is no time to measure the quick-drying dough so if the box doesn't come out right the first time, crumple the dough and try again. Turn the box and dough upside-down together, draping the dough over the box. Wet the cut edges of the dough box and then press, pinch and smooth them together at each corner, making sure they adhere. Cut the edge even all around. Leave the dough on the jar to dry.

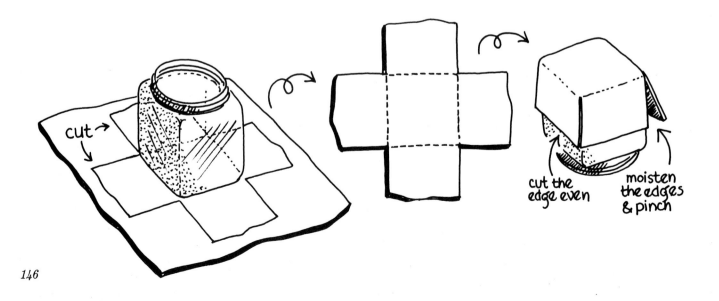

cut →

cut the edge even

moisten the edges & pinch

When the dough box seems completely dry on the outside, lift it carefully from the jar and set it right side up to dry on the inside.

Knead the leftover blue dough into a smooth ball and roll it out to ⅛″ thick. Cut the top for the dough box: Place the jar on the dough and cut a square; cut the corners off and round them a bit. Set the top aside to dry on waxed paper, turning it over every couple of hours so it dries evenly.

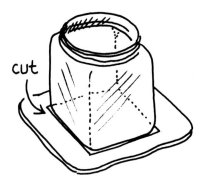

cut

MAKING THE PARTS OF THE DECORATIONS

Bird: Color one-half of the remaining white dough pink; roll it to less than ⅛″ thick and cut out four birds with the small cookie cutter. Set them aside to dry. Rewrap the leftover dough.

Petals for the flower: Make the petals in graduated colors (dark pink, medium pink, light pink, near-white pink) following these steps.

1. Color a small piece of dough dark pink. *Reminder:* The colors will dry lighter than they appear when moist. Make six or eight small dark pink petals by rolling bits of dough into ovals and pressing each one flat at one end.

2. Add a bit of white dough to the leftover dark pink and knead until well blended to make medium pink. Make eight or ten slightly larger petals.

3. Add a bit more white dough to the leftover medium pink and make ten or twelve larger petals.

4. Continue in this way until you have made the dough near-white and you have enough petals.

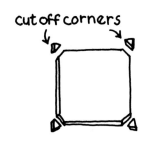

cut off corners

Arrange the petals in a flower shape to estimate if you have enough petals. Roll a dozen tiny near-white balls for the center of the flower.

Leaves: Break off a small piece of dough and color it green. Roll eight or ten small ovals and flatten them.

Birds' wings and eyes: Use the near-white dough to roll an oval and a tiny ball for each bird.

Set all the parts aside to dry on waxed paper, turning them occasionally so they dry evenly.

PUTTING THE PARTS TOGETHER

When the decorations, the box and the lid are dry, you can glue the parts together. Use a toothpick for applying glue, or use tweezers to lift parts, dip them in glue and set them in position.

Smear glue along one corner of the box, from top to bottom, and roll the corner in colored non-pareils. Repeat for the other three corners.

Glue the wings and eyes to all the birds and allow them to dry. Glue a bird to each side of the box, letting the glue dry on each side before moving on to the next side.

To make the flower on the lid, start by gluing two or three leaves to each corner. Then glue a ring of the palest (and largest) petals to the lid, overlapping the leaves. Over that, glue a ring of the next color and size of petals. Be sure that the point of each petal is tilted down and the rounded end is propped up on the previous row of petals. Continue until you have used up all your colors of petals (although you may not use up all the petals). End by gluing a little pile of tiny balls in the center of the flower. Allow the glue to dry thoroughly.

green leaves   near-white petals   light pink petals   medium pink petals   dark pink petals   tiny near-white balls

Projects for Children of All Ages

5

The projects in this chapter are fun to make for yourself and they are also particularly good for gift-giving: Say Happy Birthday to a child with Old MacDonald's Farm or treat a teenager to a necklace or a handful of Funny Pins. The miniature furniture and foods are great for kids to play with and an adult hobbyist might like to put them in a small, wood-framed shadow box to decorate a mantel or étagere.

Important: Before you set to work on any project, read the parts of Chapter 1 that deal with the kind of dough needed for that project.

Old MacDonald's Farm, page 151

Old MacDonald's Farm

You will need:

1 recipe of flour/salt dough
Rolling pin
Ruler, sharp knife
Cookie cutters: set of animals including horse, cow, dog, pig, goat, duck and chick; gingerbread man
Wooden skewers, plastic straws

Pastry cutter with scalloped blade
Acrylic paints, brushes
Polyurethane, turpentine
Package of baby rickrack

Photograph, page 150, for design and color guidance

CUTTING THE BASIC BARN, ANIMALS AND FARMER

Roll out all the dough to a large rectangle ¼″ thick. Transfer the dough carefully to the flour-dusted back of a cookie sheet. Follow the diagram to cut the barn (including windows and door) right on the cookie sheet, making sure that the barn is centered on the sheet. Use your ruler and sharp knife for the cutting.

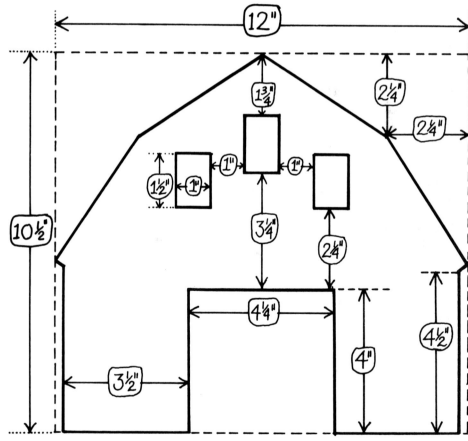

Remove the excess dough and lay it on the table. Use cookie cutters to cut out a horse, cow, dog, pig, goat, duck, chick and one gingerbread-type man. The horse (or one of the other animals, if you prefer) should fit within the barn door—check to be sure it will. Knead the remaining dough together, wrap tightly and reserve.

151

MAKING THE DETAILS ON THE BARN, ANIMALS AND FARMER

Barn: Roll some dough out to ⅛″ thick. Cut strips ½″ wide for edging the barn door. Brush water around the door, lay the strips in place and trim them to the correct size, mitering the corners as shown in the photograph. Cut strips ¼″ wide for edging the windows. Brush water around each window, lay the strips in place and trim them to the correct size as shown in the photograph. Cut out a six-pointed star, trim off the corners and incise the lines with the blunt edge of a knife. Brush water on the barn and press the star in position. Use a plastic straw to make the seven holes indicated on the diagram.

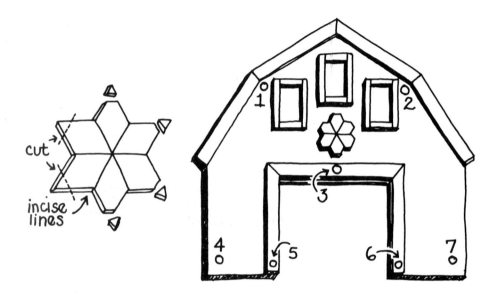

Animals: Incise eyes and mouths on all the animals and incise wings and the tailfeathers on the duck and chick. Use a plastic straw to make holes in the horse, cow, goat, dog and pig.

Farmer: Fatten up the farmer's arms with a bit of dough (use water to adhere). Push the sides of his belly in a bit and position his arms and legs as in the photograph. Cut the top of his head at an angle and add a little hand-

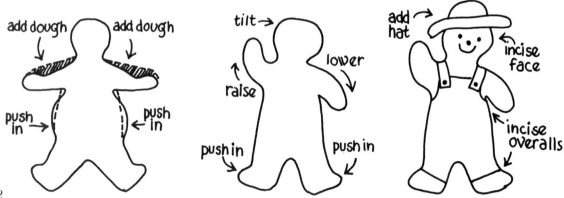

152

modeled hat, using water to secure it to his head. Incise his eyes, mouth, nose and overalls, using both the pointed and blunt ends of a wooden skewer.

ATTACHING THE ANIMALS AND FARMER TO THE BARN

Attach only the duck and chick to the barn: Brush water on the barn and press them in place as in the photograph.

Place the farmer next to the barn on the cookie sheet and cut out little bits of the barn to correspond to his hat brim, hand and foot. Brush water between the farmer and the barn and press them firmly together.

MAKING AND ATTACHING THE TREE

Roll the remaining dough into a rectangle ¼″ thick. Cut one side of the rectangle to conform to the right side of the barn. Brush the cut edge with water and butt the dough against the barn. Trim the lower edge of the rectangle even with the lower edge of the barn. Cut the tree trunk with a sharp knife, then switch to a pastry cutter to cut a free-form top for the tree. To make the leaves, use the pastry cutter to cut narrow strips of dough and then cut the strips into small sections. Brush the free-form top with water and press the leaves into position.

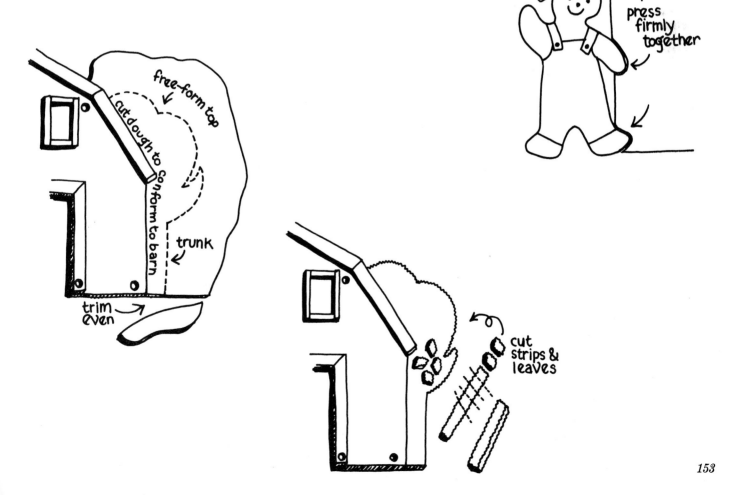

BAKING AND PAINTING THE FARM

Place the unattached animals on the cookie sheet and bake the whole farm until it is completely hard. *Note:* The unattached animals will not take as long to bake as the barn unit; keep an eye on them and remove them when they are baked. When the barn unit has baked to some hardness, run a long spatula between the barn and the cookie sheet to loosen the barn. Be very careful not to *lift* the barn with the spatula. Continue baking the barn unit until it is thoroughly hard. Remove the cookie sheet from the oven and let the barn cool on the cookie sheet. When cool, handle it carefully, picking it up by the door opening and not by any edge.

Paint the barn and all the animals white, back and front. Let the white paint dry and then apply the bright colors, following the photograph or inventing your own color scheme.

FINISHING THE FARM

When the paint has dried thoroughly, brush several coats of polyurethane on the barn unit and the unattached animals. Let each coat dry before applying the next.

The final step is to thread short loops of baby rickrack through both the holes in the barn and the holes in the unattached animals, as shown in the photograph. The ends of the rickrack may be fastened with glue or by stitching.

Miniature Furniture and Foods

You will need:

1 recipe of bread/glue dough

Food coloring

Rolling pin

Cookie cutters: plain round, about
3¼″ in diameter; plain round,
about 2¾″ in diameter; scalloped
round, 1″ to 1¼″ in diameter;
small heart, about 1⅝″ across or
use pattern given on page 156

1 stick of balsa wood, ⅜″ square,
9″ long, for table legs

1 stick of balsa wood, ¼″ square,
5½″ long, for crosspieces

1 stick of balsa wood, ¼″ square,
8¼″ long, for chair legs

Single-edge razor blade or mat
knife with new blade

Sharp knife

Jar lid about 2½″ in diameter

White glue

*Photograph, above, for design
and color guidance*

155

TABLE

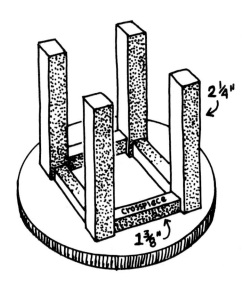

Top: Break off a four-finger-sized piece of dough and color it light brown, using red, yellow and a bit of blue food coloring. Roll the dough to ⅛″ thick and cut out a 3¼″-diameter round. Let the round dry completely, turning it occasionally so it dries evenly on both sides.

Legs: Using the single-edge blade or mat knife, cut the 9″ length of balsa into four equal pieces, each 2¼″ long. Cut the 5½″ length of balsa into four equal pieces, each 1⅜″ long. When the table top is dry, turn it wrong side up and glue the legs and crosspieces in place with white glue. Let them dry completely.

CHAIRS

Backs and seats: Break off a four-finger-sized piece of dough and color it blue (or any other color you prefer) with food coloring. Roll the dough out to ⅛″ thick and cut out four hearts, using your cookie cutter or the pattern given above (see page 18 for instructions on making and using patterns). Cut a notch in each of two hearts, as shown in the pattern, making sure the point of each unnotched heart will slip through each notch easily. Cut the points off the notched hearts, as shown in the pattern.

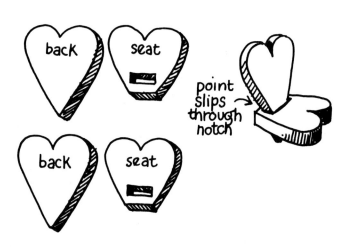

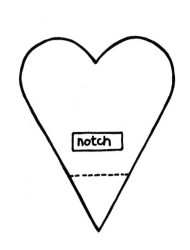

Decorate each of the chair backs with a five-petal flower and two leaves. Each petal and leaf is an oval, rolled between your fingers and flattened slightly. The center of each flower is a tiny ball, also flattened slightly. Brush the upper half of each back with water and press the petals, leaves and balls in position, referring to the photograph for placement. Allow the hearts to dry thoroughly, turning occasionally.

When the hearts are dry, glue the backs and seats together: Squeeze glue into the notch of one seat and insert the point of one flower-decorated back as far as it will go. Turn the back/seat combination over and apply more glue from the underside. Allow to dry.

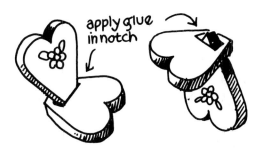

apply glue in notch

Legs: Using the single-edge blade or mat knife, cut the 8¼″ length of balsa into six equal pieces, each 1⅜″, three legs per chair. Round the square corners of the legs by carefully shaving off the corners all the way down the legs.

For each chair, cut a notch in one leg as shown, using the chair as a guide. Prop the chairs upside-down on a book and glue the legs in place. Allow to dry thoroughly.

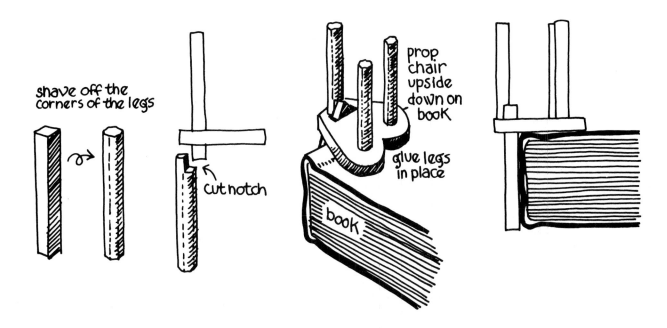

shave off the corners of the legs

cut notch

prop chair upside down on book

glue legs in place

book

VEGETABLE BASKET

Break off a small piece of dough and color it dark brown with food coloring. (Brown is made with red, yellow and a bit of blue.) Make enough brown for the rolled cookies and the cake, too.

Roll the dough to ⅛″ thick and cut out a circle about 2¾″ in diameter, using a cookie cutter. Turn the entire edge of the circle up by placing it over the jar lid and pressing the edge around the lid. Make each handle: Roll a very thin strand of dough, fold it in half and twist it. Form the twisted dough into a half circle and cut off the ends. Dab water on the edge of the basket and press the handle into place. Repeat for the second handle. Let the basket dry completely.

press edge over jar lid

VEGETABLES

Follow the directions for making vegetables in the project called Kitchen Memo Board on page 55, but make these vegetables smaller. Make one lettuce about 1¼″ in diameter, one bunch of carrots with carrots about 1″ long, three pea pods each about 1¼″ long, one ear of corn about 1¾″ long and one pumpkin about 1″ across. Allow the vegetables to dry and then arrange and glue them in the vegetable basket.

PLATE WITH APPLES

Plate: Break off and color a small piece of dough. Roll it to less than ⅛″ thick and use the small scalloped cookie cutter to cut a round. Place the round over a little pill bottle and press the scalloped edges down to form a rim. Allow to dry.

Apples: Break off and color a small piece of dough using a good amount of red coloring to make a deep pinky red (remember that the color dries darker than it appears when moist). Roll nine or ten little balls. Poke holes in the top and bottom of each ball and then shape the balls to look more like apples. Allow to dry.

When both plate and apples are dry, glue the apples in place on the plate.

shape like apples

poke holes

PLATE WITH COOKIES

Plate: Break off and color a small piece of dough. Make the plate as described above.

Cookie: Roll out one very thin rectangle of brown dough and one of uncolored dough. Brush the brown rectangle with water and place the uncolored one on top of it. Brush the uncolored rectangle with water and roll the unit up the long way. Carefully slice off cookies with a sharp knife. Allow to dry.

When both plate and cookies are dry, glue the cookies in place on the plate.

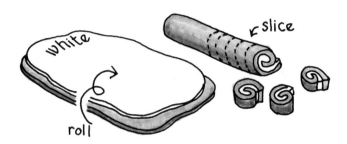

PLATE WITH CAKE

Plate: Break off and color a small piece of dough. Roll it out to less than ⅛″ thick and cut a scalloped round. Allow to dry.

Cake: Shape a small cylinder about ⅝″ in diameter and ½″ high for the cake. Press out a thin irregular round of uncolored dough and shape it over the cake to make the icing (trim it if necessary). Use the dough left from the apples to make tiny balls for the cherries on top of the cake and put the cherries in place with tiny dabs of water. Allow to dry and then glue the cake to the plate.

Hearts-and-Beads Necklace, page 161
Barrette with Bow and
Comb with Hearts and Flowers, page 163

Hearts-and-Beads Necklace

You will need:

½ recipe of bread/glue dough
Food coloring
Rolling pin
Thin nail or large needle
Heavy-duty thread, thin needle

Necklace clasp
White glue

*Photograph, page 160, for design
and color guidance*

MAKING THE BEADS

First mix all the colors of dough that you will need: Break off a finger-sized piece of dough for each color and blend in the food coloring to make red, yellow, green, blue and peach. Break off a two-finger-sized piece of dough to make yellow-green and a three-finger-sized piece to make pink. Rewrap each color tightly.

Start by making nine round pink beads. For each bead, roll a bit of dough between your palms to make a ball about ¼″ in diameter. Make holes in all nine beads: Use the thin nail or large needle to pierce the bead first from one side and then from the other. The hole must be large enough for the needle and heavy-duty thread to pass through when you string the beads.

Repeat this process to make nine beads of each color, a total of 63 beads. Set the beads aside to dry on waxed paper.

pierce in one direction
& then the other

MAKING THE HEARTS AND LEAVES

Roll the remaining pink dough to about ⅛″ to ¼″ thick. With a sharp knife, cut three small triangles. Trim them as shown and round off the edges and upper corners with your fingers. Use the thin nail or large needle to make a lateral hole in each heart, inserting the nail first from one side and then from the other.

The four leaves are formed by hand from yellow-green dough. Each leaf is about ⅛″ thick with an elongated end through which you pierce a lateral hole. Incise each leaf with a center line.

Set the hearts and leaves aside to dry on waxed paper.

elongated
end

incise a
center line

make a
lateral
hole

STRINGING THE BEADS AND ATTACHING THE CLASP

When the beads are dry, thread the thin needle with a piece of heavy-duty thread 50″ long and pull the ends of thread even to make a 25″ length. String the beads as you see them in the photograph or invent your own color arrangement. Holding the thread ends so the beads won't slip off, try on the necklace to check that the length is right for you; add more beads if needed.

Attach one half of the clasp to the *needle end* of the thread: Wrap the thread several times around the ring of the clasp, knot the thread and knot a second time. Work the needle and thread back through several beads and then snip the excess thread close to the beads. Now thread the loose ends of thread through the needle and repeat the process to attach the other half of the clasp. Put tiny dabs of white glue on the knots at each end of the necklace. Let the glue dry.

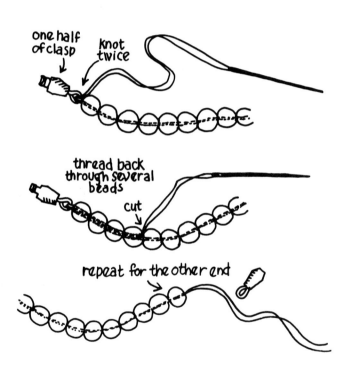

Barrette with Bow

You will need:

Small amount of bread/glue dough
Food coloring
Rolling pin
Barrette, about 3″ long

Sharp knife, ruler
Epoxy glue

*Photograph, page 160, for design
and color guidance*

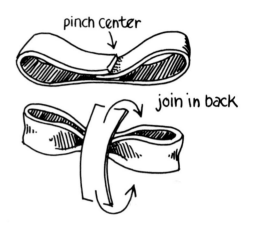

Color a small piece of dough and roll it out to about 1/16″ thick. With a sharp knife, cut one strip 5″ x 1/2″, another strip 3¼″ x 1/2″ and a third strip 1″ long and a little less than 1/2″ wide.

Shape the 5″ strip into a bow as shown and adhere the ends to the center with dabs of water. Pinch the joint slightly narrower than the bow. Roll the 1″ strip even thinner and wrap it around the center of the bow, securing it at the back with a dab of water and cutting off any excess strip.

Cut notches in the ends of the 3¼″ strip. Brush the strip with water and center the bow on it. Bend the ends of the strip slightly downward. Allow the dough to dry, making sure the bow stays open and doesn't sag closed and flat. When it is almost dry, turn it over so the underside can dry, too.

Glue the bow to the barrette with epoxy. Let the glue dry overnight.

Comb with Hearts and Flowers

You will need:

Small amount of bread/glue dough
Food coloring
Rolling pin
Comb

Epoxy glue

*Photograph, page 160, for design
and color guidance*

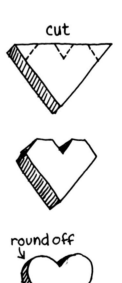

Color small amounts of dough pink, blue, green and yellow. Roll the pink dough to 1/8″ thick and make the hearts by cutting out three triangles of dough as shown. They should fit across the comb, leaving a slight amount of room at each end. Round off the upper edges of the hearts.

Decorate each heart with tiny flowers and leaves: The petals are tiny ovals rolled between your fingers; the leaves are tiny ovals flattened slightly. Roll tiny balls for the center. Brush the heart with water and gently press the petals, centers and leaves in place. Center the hearts on the bar of the comb. Roll blue balls to fit between the hearts and at each end of the bar. Leave all the pieces on the comb to dry so they retain the shape of the comb.

When the pieces are thoroughly dry, lift each heart and ball, apply epoxy glue to the space each occupied on the comb and replace the heart and ball on the glue. Allow the epoxy to dry overnight.

Funny Pins, below
Rose Pins, page 166

Funny Pins

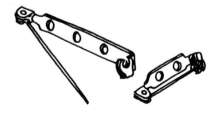

½ recipe of bread/glue dough
Food coloring
Rolling pin
Cookie cutters: small pig; tiny chick;
   tiny duck
Garlic press
Pin-backs: 1¼" long for the pig; 1"
   long for the carrots; ¾" long for the
   duck, chick or watermelon

Epoxy glue
Polyurethane, turpentine, brush
   (optional)

*Photograph, above, for design
and color guidance*

Note: Any of the pins (when completely dry) may be brushed with polyurethane for a slightly glossy look.

PINK PIG PIN

With food coloring, color a small amount of dough pink. Roll the dough out to ⅛" thick and use the cookie cutter to cut out a pig. Add a tiny little piece of dough to the tail and curl it around. Cut the mouth with a sharp knife and make the eye with a black pen. Allow to dry, turning occasionally so the underside dries, too. Glue the pin-back on with epoxy and let it dry overnight.

CARROT PIN

Color a small amount of dough orange and a small amount yellow-green. Model three carrots (each about 1" to 1¼") by hand and use a bit of water to attach them to each other at the tops. Force the yellow-green dough through a garlic press to make the leaves; use a sharp knife to lift the dough from the press. Brush the tops of the carrots with water and position the leaves on the tops. Be sure they stick securely. Lay the completed carrots on a surface and press gently to flatten the underside. Allow to dry thoroughly before gluing the pin-back on with epoxy.

WATERMELON PIN

Color small amounts of dough green, pink and purple. Roll the pink dough to ⅛" thick and cut out a half-circle 1" in diameter. Brush water on the curved edge of the half-circle and add a band of green dough to make the rind of the melon, cutting the green off neatly at the top edge. Roll tiny bits of purple for the seeds and apply them to the pink with tiny dots of water. Allow the watermelon to dry thoroughly and then glue the pin-back in place with epoxy glue.

CHICK-IN-THE-GRASS PIN

Color small amounts of dough yellow, yellow-green and orange. Roll the yellow to ⅛" thick and use the cookie cutter to cut out a chick. Add a tiny orange eye and beak to the chick. To make the grass, force yellow-green dough through a garlic press until the strands are about ¼" long. Run a sharp knife across the press to lift the group of strands off and then gently mold them together into a little patch of grass. Brush the bottom of the chick with water and tuck it into the grass. Allow the chick-in-the-grass to dry thoroughly. Glue the pin-back to the back of the chick with epoxy. Let the epoxy dry overnight.

DUCK-IN-A-POND PIN

Color small amounts of dough yellow, orange and blue. Roll the yellow to ⅛" thick and use the cookie cutter to cut out a duck. Add a tiny orange eye and bill and a tiny white wing to the duck. Model a little boat-shaped blue pond to fit the duck. Brush the bottom edge of the duck with water and press the duck onto the pond. Allow the duck-in-a-pond to dry thoroughly. Use epoxy to glue the pin-back to the back of the duck. Let the epoxy dry overnight.

Rose Pins

You will need:

Small amount of bread/glue dough

Food coloring

Rolling pin

Small round cutter ¾″ to 1″ in
diameter (the cap of a medicine
bottle or pill container will do)

Pin-backs: ½″ long for a pin with
one rose; ¾″ or 1″ long for a pin
with two roses •

Epoxy glue

Polyurethane, turpentine, brush
(optional)

*Photograph, page 164, for design
and color guidance*

HOW TO MAKE A ROSE

Roll bread/glue dough very thin and cut out several circles with a small
round cutter. Roll one circle tightly to form the center bud of the rose.
Brush water along the lower part of a second circle and roll it around the
bud, pinching it at the stem end to secure it. Take a third circle and flatten
it out even more to make an oval. Brush water along the lower edge of the
oval and wrap it around the rose, partly overlapping the previous petal.
Pinch it at the stem end. Continue adding oval petals in this manner until
the rose is the size you want. Bend the outer petals open slightly to look
more like a real rose. When all the petals have been pinched on securely at
the stem end, carefully cut off the excess dough to form a flat bottom.

 roll one circle
 wrap another circle around
 wrap an oval around
 wrap another oval around
 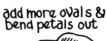 add more ovals & bend petals out

MAKING THE ROSE PIN

Color a small piece of dough and make roses according to the directions
above. If you are making a two-rose pin, place the two roses next to each
other and join with a dab of water. *Tip:* Consider making roses with two
colors of dough—dark pink bud and light pink petals, peach bud and yellow
petals, pale pink bud and lavender petals.

Shape some small leaves by hand and attach them with water to the
underside of the rose or roses. Keep the underside as flat as possible. Allow
the roses to dry, then turn them over to let the undersides dry, too.

Reminder: If you prefer a glossier finish, brush the completely dry roses
with a coat of polyurethane.

Use epoxy to glue a pin-back to the flat underside of each rose or pair of
roses. Allow the epoxy to dry overnight.

INDEX